P9-DSV-168

A PORTION OF THAT FIELD

GWENDOLYN BROOKS

OTTO KERNER

ALLAN NEVINS

PAUL M. ANGLE

MARK VAN DOREN

PAUL H. DOUGLAS

BRUCE CATTON

ADLAI E. STEVENSON

A Portion of That Field

The Centennial of the Burial of Lincoln

UNIVERSITY OF ILLINOIS PRESS

Urbana, Chicago, and London, 1967

Manufactured in the United States of America
Library of Congress Catalog Card No. 67-12993

Civil War Centennial Commission of Illinois

Contents

In the Time of Detachment, in the Time of Cold

1965

BY GWENDOLYN BROOKS

The good man.
He is still enhancer, renouncer.
In the time of detachment,
In the time of the vivid heathen and affectionate evil,
In the time of oral
Grave grave legalities of hate — all real
Walks our prime registered reproach and seal!
Our successful moral.
The good man.

Watches our bogus roses, our rank wreath, our
Love's unreliable cement, the gray
Jubilees of our demondom.
                                                  Coherent
Counsel! Good man! Good Lincoln! Abraham! —
Require of us our terribly excluded blue!
Constrain, repair your ripped, revolted land.
Put hand in hand land over.
Reprove
The abler droughts and manias of the day
And a felicity entreat.
Love.
Complete
Your pledges, reinforce your aides, renew
Stance, testament.

Or
Force our poor sense unto your logics! lend
Superlatives and prudence: to extend
Our judgment — through the terse and diesel day;
To
Singe! smite! beguile our own bewilderments away.
Teach barterers the money of your star!
Or
Retrieve our trade from out the bad bazaar.

In the time of detachment, in the time of cold, in this time
Tutor our difficult sunlight. Rouse our rhyme.

"We Are Not Enemies but Friends. . . ."

BY GOVERNOR OTTO KERNER

Precisely one hundred years ago this morning, at 8:40 A.M. to be exact, Abraham Lincoln returned to Springfield for the last time. He had been gone four years, two months, and twenty-three days since that rainy morning of February 11, 1861, when he bid farewell to his friends and neighbors at the Great Western Station. His farewell to Springfield was a characteristically simple yet eloquent, brief address, which began, "No one, not in my situation, can appreciate my feelings of sadness at this parting."

En route to Washington he stopped and spoke at many places, including Independence Hall, where on February 22 — George Washington's birthday — in referring to the noble act performed in that historic structure a century before, he said: "It was that which gave promise that in due time the weights should be lifted from the shoulders of all men, and that *all* should have an equal chance. This is the sentiment embodied in that Declaration of Independence."

Then he continued in awesome prophecy, "Can this country be saved upon that basis? If it can, I will consider myself one of the happiest men in the world if I can help save it. . . . But, if this country cannot be saved without giving up that principle — I was about to say I would rather be assassinated on this spot than to surrender it."

He had also referred to this theme on the previous day, when he addressed the New Jersey Senate at Trenton. He spoke of the Revolutionary War soldiers and told how, as a boy, his reading of Parson Weem's *Life of George Washington* had stirred him, particularly the accounts of the fortitude and sacrifice of the fighting men. Forty years later, he could say, "I recollect thinking then, boy even though I was, that there must have been something more than common that those men struggled for."

And the boy, become a man and about to assume the office as President of the United States, went on to say: "I am exceedingly anxious that that thing which they struggled for; that something even more than National Independence; that something that held out a great promise to all the people of the world to all time to come . . . shall be perpetuated in accordance with the original idea for which that struggle was made, and I shall be most happy indeed if I shall be an humble instrument in the hands of the Almighty, and of this his almost chosen people, for perpetuating the object of that great struggle."

This statement by Abraham Lincoln contains the gist of his political philosophy. It also reveals the most impelling quality of his personal philosophy. For in the intervening years since boyhood he had thought deeply about the true meaning of our War of Independence. And he had concluded that in the great human document that it inspired and in the form of government which had been erected on the principles of that great document were to be found the means of bringing peace, prosperity, and happiness to what he called, "the whole great family of man."

Lincoln was so dedicated to this idea that he could say in 1861, "I have never had a feeling politically which did not spring from the sentiments embodied in the Declaration of Independence."

It annoyed Lincoln when Americans, especially in celebrating the Fourth of July, seemed satisfied to look upon the Declaration of Independence as merely a justification and glorification of their separation from England. He had thought, he said, that it promised Americans more than the rights of British subjects under new lords and masters. To him the heart of the Declaration was the assertions that all men are created equal and that they are entitled to life, liberty, and the pursuit of happiness, and in its avowal that the just purpose of human government is to make those rights realities.

On Monday, March 4, 1861, shortly after noon, Abraham Lincoln appeared on the east portico of the Capitol of the United States, to deliver his Inaugural Address and take the oath of office as the sixteenth President of the United States.

By the time he spoke, seven states, extending from South Carolina to Texas, had formally voted in state conventions to secede from the Union. They had formed a new republic, the Confederate States of America, and had inaugurated Jefferson Davis of Mississippi to be their president just ten days before. The secessionists had taken over all of the federal functions and had seized forts and arsenals. In the lower South only two forts remained in federal hands.

What could Lincoln do in this situation? The southerners thought he should let them go, and there were even some northerners who felt that this was the easiest solution to the problem. But the man speaking in front of the Capitol did not belive this. He said that under the Constitution "the Union of these States is perpetual."

Moreover he felt deep conviction that if the cause of union should fail in the United States it would be a blow to the cause of democracy throughout the world. The world must be shown that democracy did not mean weakness. He asked, "Why should there not be a patient confidence in the ultimate justice of the people? Is there any better, or equal hope, in the world?"

He pleaded with the people of the South to come back into the Union. He could speak to them as a southerner. He understood their problems, but he could see the complete picture and the greater cause. As he came to the end of his inaugural, he again reminded the entire nation that we had a great common heritage: "We are not enemies, but friends. We must not be enemies. Though passion may have strained, it must not break our bonds of affection. The mystic chords of memory, stretching from every battle-field, and patriot grave, to every living heart and hearthstone, all over this broad land, will yet swell the chorus of the Union, when again touched, as surely they will be, by the better angels of our nature."

It is one of the ironies of history that to the gentlest and most peace-loving of our Presidents fell the lot of committing the nation to a brothers' war — one of the bloodiest wars in history. How often he must silently have prayed: "Father, if it be Thy will, let this cup pass from me." Yet in his dedication to the American experiment, he drank the cup's full measure and became, himself, part of the sacrifice because to him the breakup of the Union meant death to democracy and hopelessness for the world.

No twisting or distortion of the evidence is required to prove that this was Lincoln's conception of the war. Very early in the struggle he explained to his young secretary, John Hay, "For my part, I consider the central idea pervading this struggle is the necessity that is upon us of proving that popular government is not an absurdity. We must settle the question now, whether in a free government the minority have the right to break up the government whenever they choose. If we fail it will go far to prove the incapability of the people to govern themselves."

Throughout the war, in one crisis after another, Lincoln took people into his confidence. And when he had finished summing up a situation in plain, simple language that everyone could understand, there were no loose ends dangling, and he had covered the matter with such sure logic that usually the people agreed that his course should be their course.

To be sure there were times when Lincoln failed, notably when the people refused to heed his plea for the maintenance of the Union, and when the people of the border slave states rejected his appeal to abolish slavery with a grant-in-aid for slaveholders from the federal government.

But it is these very failures that put a democratic leader to the test. For when the people refuse to see things as he sees them, his faith in the people must surpass his faith in himself. Otherwise he becomes cynical and useless as a leader, or he takes refuge in the autocratic conception of government as a means of giving the people, not what they want, but what he thinks is good for them.

Thus the American presidential office, or a governor's office, is no place for a theorist — he must be a practical leader. But to the rigid mind of the doctrinaire — one who believes his theories are beyond dispute — to compromise an issue is to compromise himself. The idealist will lose the whole loaf rather than be satisfied with half of it, whereas the successful politician learns to be content with whatever part of his program he can get, and hopes to get more later.

The quality of restraint in Lincoln was an element of his greatness. Without compromising his inner convictions, he had the patience to put himself in the right place and then wait for the march of time and the propitious circumstance to find him there.

A century ago this tall lawyer from Illinois believed that more could be accomplished by meeting as friends, not as enemies. Unfortunately, we tried, as enemies, to solve a problem that confronted this nation. The cost was terrible, and in the end it was by peaceful means that the purposes of democracy were best served. There are forces that cannot be stopped. The natural aspiration of man to better himself and the struggle for human freedom and social justice will probably go on to the end of time. The only permanent advance mankind can hope for must be made in the mind and consciousness of man himself.

Robert E. Lee, who knew all too well the horrors of war, saw hope only in the peaceful approach. Writing shortly after the Civil War he said: "All should unite in honest efforts to obliterate the effects of the war and to restore the blessings of peace. They should . . . promote harmony and good feeling . . . and elect . . .

wise and patriotic men, who will devote their abilities to the interests of the country and the healing of all dissensions."

Lincoln hated the institution of slavery for many reasons, but one of his main reasons was that it "enables the enemies of free institutions, with plausibility, to taunt us as hypocrites."

The same reasoning applies to us today. All of us, in every section of the country, are confronted with pressing problems, the solutions of which are the concern not just of our own community or nation, but of the entire world. Let us not supply the enemies of democracy with arguments that might enable them to taunt us as hypocrites.

Abraham Lincoln had the answer a century ago. His words are just as meaningful, perhaps more meaningful, today. "If there ever could be a time for mere catch arguments, that time surely is not now. In times like the present, men should utter nothing for which they would not willingly be responsible through time in eternity."

As friends and neighbors, let us face our responsibility and perform in good faith and with honor the tasks required of us.

Where We Stand: Civil War Scholarship

BY ALLAN NEVINS

The burly, sharp-eyed superintendent of the newspaper section of the British Museum Library in Colindale, a London suburb, eyed me sharply as I put in a slip requesting some materials on Lord Palmerston's Ministry. "Haven't you chaps almost finished the writing of your Civil War history?" he demanded. "I thought you were to complete it this spring. And yet we have four men working here right now on your eternal Civil War." He grinned genially. I assured him that the writing of Civil War history was just beginning, not ending. "My dear sir," I said, "in my opinion the most important part of our Civil War history remains to be penned." And this opinion I verily hold valid.

It better behooves us to look forward than back; to speak of what remains undone than of what has been completed. It is a long, long time since William Swinton wrote perhaps the first important piece of Civil War history; it is a hundred years lacking only a few months. General Jacob D. Cox relates in his reminiscences that while campaigning in West Virginia in 1861 he was joined by two newspaper correspondents, who requested to be taken into his mess as volunteer aides with military rank. He refused. Thereupon they said: "Very well, General Cox thinks he can get along without us, but we will show him. We will write him down." They did publish libelous letters about him and his army. One of these men was the *New York Times* correspondent, William Swinton. Ulysses S. Grant writes in his *Personal Memoirs* that during the Virginia campaign of 1864 one of his staff pulled a newspaperman out of a hiding place where he was listening to a conference between Grant and George Meade. He was this same William Swinton. Yet Swinton was a man of talent who became the first important military historian of the Civil War. He wrote a book, *Campaigns of the Army of the Potomac* (1866), and another, *The Twelve Decisive Battles of the War,* that possess some enduring values.

A far more important military historian than Swinton, Louis Phillippe Albert d'Orléans, Comte de Paris, began publishing his history of the war ninety years ago.

After serving for a time on George McClellan's staff, he had returned home to give prolonged study to every phase of the conflict. His ten volumes in French, immediately translated into English in four volumes, united comprehensiveness, clarity, and objectivity. One commendable feature of the work is that while he gives full credit to West Point and the regular army, he makes it clear that the main burden of all operations falls upon the volunteer and drafted forces — particularly the volunteers. It is another of his merits that although he gives unstinted praise to Robert E. Lee, he regards Grant and William T. Sherman as the outstanding military chieftains of the conflict.

Swinton and the Comte de Paris were followed eighty-five years ago by the commencement of the most massive compilation of military sources ever issued in any land. The first volumes of the 130 which were termed *The Official Records of the Union and Confederate Armies* appeared in 1880. The principal credit for beginning this work must go to Edward Davis Townsend, a Massachusetts man who was adjutant general to Winfield Scott in 1861, and the next year became adjutant general of the United States, a post akin to that of chief of staff — if the term "staff" was then known. He labored throughout the war in close relationship to Secretary of War Edwin Stanton and President Lincoln, performing important services of which the public was quite unaware. Historians should never forget that soon after the conflict, Townsend issued his momentous order for the collection of all war papers, North and South, thus laying a foundation for the *Official Records*. He also gathered newspaper materials. How often, in my Columbia years, I gazed with respect at his tremendous collection of Civil War scrapbooks, full of useful clippings, in the Columbia Library.

Then the stream of military history broadened. In 1881 Scribner's began publishing their series of green-bound volumes called *The Campaigns of the Civil War*, of which the longest, *The Virginia Campaigns,* by the engineer Andrew A. Humphreys, is an acknowledged classic. In 1884 the *Century Magazine* began the great collection of articles by participants later gathered into four well-illustrated volumes under the title *Battles and Leaders of the Civil War*. It had hardly been digested by readers when a new landmark in the field of military history began to emerge in 1894, John Codman Ropes then publishing the first volume of his *Story of the Civil War*; a work which, as he said, had a novel aim — "to write on the subjects treated from the standpoint of each of the contending parties." Ropes, born of an old Massachusetts family and educated at Harvard, had been prevented by physical disability from joining the Union armies. However, he was a passionate student of military affairs, as his wartime correspondence with John Chipman Gray shows. After the war he helped found the Military Historical Society of Massachusetts (1876), wrote a number of military monographs, and had brought out the second volume of his full-dress history when death stopped his pen in 1898.

The flood of Civil War history, thus loosed, has continued in unabated volume ever since. Particularly has it grown in strength during the recent commemorative years. Writes the British historian Marcus Cunliffe: "For whatever combination of reasons, Centennial writing has dealt mainly with combat. Military history, to choose the most suitable cliché, has had a field day." This is true. Any objective observer of commemorative writing in the past four years must make two comments. The first will record astonishment at the sheer volume of work turned out. Dwight McDonald of the *New Yorker* classifies all American books of the period in three groups: fiction, nonfiction, and Civil War publications. Forty-four state commissions, a dozen city commissions, and a national commission have all been busy. A score of publishers, led by the Indiana University Press, have worked like beavers. Scholars in cohorts and journalists in battalions have moved to the charge. The second comment of any impartial observer will record gratification or regret over the fact that nearly all of those books, monographs, and articles have been upon military subjects. A word recently creeping into general use in modern journalism is "redundancy"; redundancy in machines, redundancy in products, redundancy in labor. All other forms of redundancy sink into insignificance compared with the redundancy in Civil War military books.

We have had compilations of military diaries and letters in thickening numbers; biographies of army leaders, naval leaders, calvary and artillery leaders; books about war correspondents, war spies, war heroines, and, we may be thankful, even some war privates; volumes about campaigns, about battles, about skirmishes, about this or that single military episode. For the best, and some have been very good, we may be grateful. Still, we feel a sense of surfeit. It was the conviction that drum and trumpet history was beginning to deafen us that led St. Clair McKelway to pen his stirring narrative of the engagement at Tuckertee Ridge. Readers who after a million pages of battle have felt themselves suffocating in quicksands of tactical detail hailed his account of "an all-purpose Civil War battle" with the hope that coming historians might substitute it for intended new records of Gettysburg, Chickamauga, or the Wilderness. Why go into all that for the thousandth time? Why not simply agree on Tuckertee Ridge?

Just before dusk, a strange gray shape rounded the bend at Beulah's Gulch. It was the *Merrimac*. Admiral Porter scuttled the gantlet. Jubal Early fell back. Stuart fell forward and sounded his bugles. At last, the dynamite charges in the tunnel under Jackson were detonated. But Jackson's sentinels had already carried him to Joab's Farm on the double. Rosecrans straddled Pemberton. Grant threw out Burnside. Lee threw out Bragg. Meade walked. McClellan redoubled as Mosby's irregulars rode through Hapgood Junction, delaying all northbound trains for forty minutes. Many stragglers panicked. Longstreet wheeled north on the Warrenton Turnpike to keep his memorable rendezvous with destiny.

The kind of history thus satirized has often combined the aridity of the pedant with the colloquialism of the sports writer. One foreign critic writes that, reading it, he has been tempted to wonder whether military history really is a branch of scholarship. "It seems to me," he says, "a kind of hobby, akin to solving jigsaw puzzles and collecting toy soldiers. The Civil War, over the past few years, had threatened to turn into the Civil War Game."

We must not be unfair. The biographies of G. F. R. Henderson on Stonewall Jackson and Douglas Freeman on Lee; the book of Major John Bigelow on Chancellorsville and narrative by General Morris Schaff on the Wilderness; the description by Frank A. Haskell of the fighting at Gettysburg (to name only the work of dead authors), can never be forgotten. We have recent books as good. They are sterling history, and what is more, they occasionally contain passages that rise to the height of literature. And yet we may justifiably feel that the military side of the Civil War has been overdone; that after so much of it every fresh addition should be regarded with suspicion; and that it is high time the balance was redressed by more attention to the other aspects of the vast epic struggle.

The Civil War was a many-sided convulsion. It was a cosmic drama too vast, too multitudinous in its aspects, to be fitted into any single category. It is partly because so much attention has been paid to guns, swords, and battlesmoke that historians have never really caught its many-sided significance in the story of the development of the American people. Much of its true history remains to be written. Only when it is properly analyzed and recorded will people begin to comprehend what a great frame it fills, and what a rich meaning it holds.

As Walt Whitman wrote, it was too big a subject for any book or shelf of books.

"Of that many threaded drama," wrote Whitman, "with its sudden and strange surprises, its confounding of prophecies, its moments of despair, the dread of foreign interference, the interminable campaigns, the bloody battles, the mighty and cumbrous and green armies, the drafts and bounties — the immense money expenditures, like a heavy-pouring constant rain — with, over the whole land, the last three years of the struggle, an unending, universal mourning wail of women, parents, orphans — the marrow of the tragedy concentrated in these army hospitals . . . [all this forms] the untold and unwritten history of the war, infinitely greater, like life's, than the few scraps and distortions that are ever told or written."

It is the social, the economic, the civil, the cultural, and the psychological aspects of the struggle that have thus far been neglected. America was changed in these four years as completely as the materials in a Bessemer furnace are changed from a mass of ore and coal into a bar of steel. It was transformed. An astute British observer, writing from New Haven, Connecticut, on the Fourth of July following the assassination of Lincoln, set forth the fact of this transformation in vigorous language. The Americans, he wrote, had learned a great lesson:

The Americans have now for the first time become fully aware of the greatness of their own power; but they have learnt at the same time how much of sorrow and anxiety and suffering it costs a nation to exert its full strength. The whole land is rejoicing today. There comes into my window, as I write in this quiet New England town, the sound of bells, of cannonade, of fusillade, of cheering, and of every other token of public joy. But the most enthusiastic of all those who are cheering and firing guns today now knows what he never knew before, what the horrors of war mean, what sort of scene a battlefield is, what kind of customer a determined enemy is, how much money it takes to feed and clothe an army for even a few months. He remembers, too, very vividly, how people felt last summer, while Sherman was still on his march through Atlanta, and while Grant was struggling through the Wilderness; and what sort of sensation it was, to go further back, which the public felt when the news came of the repulses of Chancellorsville and Fredericksburg, or when it woke up and read in the papers that gold had stood at 280.

In fact, if I may judge from what I have read, there is much the same difference between the America of today and the America of four years ago that there is between a man at 21 and at 35. There is an increased sense of power, an increased confidence in the principles by which the national life is regulated, a very much diminished sensibility to foreign criticism; but there is also an increased feeling of responsibility with regard to both words and deeds, a stronger sense than ever of the difficulty of cutting a great figure in the world, or of achieving really great results, and a perception of the politic value of simple justice which I think I may fairly say the war has not only developed, but almost created.

It is this history of the re-creation, the transformation of America in the four Civil War years, the history of its growth from callow and uncertain youth to robust and confident manhood, that remains to be written. And this is a theme beside which the penning of addenda to our military history dwindles into superfluity and pales into insignificance.

A few, but a very few, of the great wartime changes behind the battlefront have been well treated. In attention to economic, social, and civil history southern writers have stood in advance of their northern compeers; they have dealt with a few problems in quite conclusive terms. Frank Owsley, for example, conclusively settled the question of the injury done the Confederacy by states' rights. He showed how the refusal of the states to surrender their supplies of arms at the beginning of the war kept the Confederate armies down to 400,000 men when they might have had 600,000, and how in the last year of the war state selfishness kept the veterans under Lee and Joe Johnston ragged and hungry when they might have been adequately clothed and fed. Thus, too, Charles W. Ramsdell effectively settled the question of the injury done the South by bad financial policies. In his book *Behind the Lines in the Southern Confederacy* he assessed the effect of a flood of paper money in not merely sapping the power of the government to buy, but in destroying all internal security.

The economic and social changes in the North, however, were far more sweeping and profound than in the South. When shall we have an adequate assessment of them, expert in terms of modern psychology, economics, and sociology? It is this question that makes it clear that we have not finished the writing of our true Civil War history; we have just embarked upon it. This spring has witnessed the publication in Great Britain of a remarkable book upon the history of World War I, a volume that in its way may almost be called epochal. It is a work entitled *Deluge*, written by the journalist Arthur Marwick. Mr. Marwick does not address himself to the oft-told story of the origins of World War I; the story of how Britain and the other European nations were sucked into a monstrous, brutal, and obscenely destructive conflict. He does not relate again the oft-told story of battles and the campaigns of Gallipoli and the Somme. What he does is to show how the Great War, which was indeed a deluge that swept away half the ancient landmarks of Britain, altered every aspect of national life, so that everything, from the class structure of the land to the patterns of consumption and the character of industry and labor, was transformed.

When shall we have an adequate study of the growth of organization in the United States during the Civil War years? When shall we have studies explaining why most Americans emerged from the conflict with more mature ideas, with a keener sense of the importance of social change, and with a fuller understanding of the difficulty of drawing great results from reform? When shall we understand what the war did for the position of women, what innovations it brought in culture, and what alterations it produced in the treatment of poverty and crime, of disease and public health? When shall we comprehend, as Lincoln did, that the war inevitably produced changes in party ideas and outlooks that gave us in effect totally new parties? The United States in 1870 was a nation quite different from the United States of 1860, and the forces that made it different are now far more worthy of study than battles or battle leaders. The *Impact Series* that the National Commission has launched will give the systematic restudy of the war the start it needs; and certainly this sweeping restudy must be carried forward on an ever broadening front and with ever deepening techniques.

Where We Stand: Lincoln Scholarship

BY PAUL M. ANGLE

It has become customary — indeed, almost obligatory — for the writer of any serious paper on Abraham Lincoln to open with a reference to James G. Randall's article, "Has the Lincoln Theme Been Exhausted?," which appeared in the *American Historical Review* for January, 1936. Many of you will remember, I am sure, that Randall's answer was an emphatic "No!"

For this conclusion Randall had good reasons. First of all, he pointed to the lack of a comprehensive and competently edited collection of Lincoln's writings and speeches. The writings of Lincoln's close associates, in published form, left much to be desired. The important diary of John Hay had been "printed but not published" with all surnames represented only by dashes. The identity of the author of "The Diary of a Public Man," as well as the authenticity of the work, were unsettled questions. The famous diary of Gideon Welles, in print for years, had been shown to contain many interpolations, but the need for a critical edition had not been met. Only fragments of the Civil War diaries of Salmon P. Chase had been published, and these with little of the editorial comment they deserved.

Important collections of manuscripts remained closed to scholars. The Robert Todd Lincoln Papers were impounded in the Library of Congress and would not be opened for a dozen years. The Herndon-Weik Papers were still in private hands, as were the papers of David Davis, Richard Yates, and William H. Seward.

Randall surveyed the field of Lincoln literature and found it woefully lacking. To enumerate the lacunae in detail would be tedious, yet it may be mentioned that he called for an adequate Lincoln bibliography, for a study of the biographers of Lincoln and of Herndon in particular, and for a new life of Lincoln, "up-to-date in its use of sources and monographs, and full-length in its scope." As Randall saw the field, the greatest opportunities for original work were to be encountered in the presidential period of Lincoln's life. Among subjects awaiting thorough investigation were the Radicals, the Sumter question, Lincoln's relations with Congress, the War Governors, and wartime propaganda.

Twenty-nine years have passed since Randall's provocative essay was published — time enough for us to ask the question, "How does Lincoln scholarship stand today?"

To begin with, we have a comprehensive and competently edited collection of Lincoln's writings and speeches. (I mention this first not only because it is by long odds the most important contribution of the last generation, but also because it originated with and was carried to completion by the Abraham Lincoln Association of this city.) *The Collected Works of Abraham Lincoln* cannot be said to be complete — no collection ever can be — but the chance of truly important unpublished letters turning up is remote. One knowledgeable dealer can think of no more than half a dozen that have come to light since the *Collected Works* was published in 1953. And I believe we can say with assurance that no letter, now unknown, will change the Lincoln record in any important particular.

As far as the basic writings of Lincoln's contemporaries are concerned, all except one of Randall's desiderata have been supplied. We now have scholarly editions of the Hay, Welles, and Chase diaries. Only "The Diary of a Public Man" continues to present baffling problems, but in the light of the exhaustive work done by F. Lauriston Bullard and Frank Maloy Anderson, I doubt that these problems will ever be solved. I might add that we have at least two bonuses in contemporary diaries of which Randall was unaware: *The Journal of Benjamin Moran,* secretary of the American legation in

London during the Civil War, and the *Diary of George Templeton Strong,* New York lawyer and guiding spirit of the United States Sanitary Commission. Neither has the degree of relevance to the life of Lincoln that marks the diaries of his close associates, but each yields returns of consequence.

All the important collections of manuscripts that Randall found closed are now freely available: the Robert Todd Lincoln Papers and the Herndon-Weik Papers in the Library of Congress; the papers of David Davis and those of Richard Yates in the Illinois State Historical Library; and the papers of William H. Seward at the University of Rochester. Again, scholars have a bonus which Randall did not foresee in two collections recently acquired by the Huntington Library: the papers of Hiram Barney, the Republican leader whom Lincoln appointed Collector of the Port of New York; and the very large collection of S. L. M. Barlow, New York lawyer and Democratic politician.

In the general field of Lincoln literature nearly all the gaps that Randall pointed out have been filled. We have an adequate Lincoln bibliography, that of Jay Monaghan. However, twenty years have passed since publication, and a supplementary volume will soon be called for. We have Benjamin P. Thomas' fine study of the Lincoln biographers and David Donald's definitive life of William H. Herndon. We have not one but two excellent biographies: Thomas' *Abraham Lincoln* and Carl Sandburg's one-volume *Abraham Lincoln: The Prairie Years and the War Years*, published in 1954. (I specify this title quite carefully because I consider it to be far superior to the original six volumes from which it was condensed.) Moreover, the presidential period has been worked over thoroughly — by Randall himself in *Lincoln the President* and by Allan Nevins in volumes one and two of his still unfinished *The War for the Union*. In addition, numerous monographs of the highest merit have appeared. I cite only a few when I mention David M. Potter's *Lincoln and His Party in the Secession Crisis*, Kenneth M. Stampp's *And the War Came*, William B. Hesseltine's *Lincoln and the War Governors*, T. Harry Williams' *Lincoln and His Generals*, and *Lincoln and the Patronage* by Harry J. Carmin and Reinhard H. Luthin.

Nor is this all. When Randall wrote, there were only two studies of Lincoln as a lawyer, both superficial. Now we have two more books, both first-rate, devoted to that subject alone, and several others which touch on it in considerable part. In January, 1936, only one volume of the series of day-by-day records of Lincoln's life, sponsored by the Abraham Lincoln Association, had been published. The series was completed in 1941, and revised and enlarged to include the presidential years by the Lincoln Sesquicentennial Commission in 1960. The letters of Stephen A. Douglas have been published and so has a modern edition of the Lincoln-Douglas debates.

I think we may now answer Randall's question. The Lincoln theme, if not exhausted, is becoming very, very tired.

The recent output of Lincoln books supports this conclusion. I can think of several in which the material for a short paper embodying original research or new interpretation has been blown up to three hundred pages. I can also think of three books whose authors could, with charity, be characterized as incompetent, but who really deserve a harsher epithet, dishonest. The law of libel being what it is, I shall go no further. But I fear that we shall see more of this kind of thing — more inflated books, incompetent books, dishonest books — in the future.

Assuming then, as I think we may, that for all practical purposes the record is complete, what remains to be said of Lincoln?

Every present-day historian's vocabulary includes two words: "interpretation" and "reinterpretation." I am not sure that I can define them with the finality of *Webster's International* — if indeed, in the light of the Third Edition, that once-supreme arbiter still possesses finality — but I shall try. In my understanding, to interpret is to deduce meaning from a sequence of facts; to reinterpret is to deduce a new and different meaning from the same set of facts.

Sometimes it seems to me that interpretation and reinterpretation are mere games played by historians pursuing an easy avenue to publication. But there are other times when interpretation, and particularly reinterpretation, are desirable. Times change, standards change. It may be unfair to assess the meaning of a man's life by any standards other than those that prevailed in his own time, but it is inevitable that an assessment will be made from the viewpoint of the present.

Lincoln's attitude toward the Negro is a case in point. To many Negroes today Lincoln is not the hero he once was. They know that in the course of the Lincoln-Douglas debates he asserted flatly:

> I am not nor ever have been in favor of bringing about in any way the social and political equality of the white and black races — that I am not nor ever have been in favor of making voters or jurors of Negroes, nor of qualifying them to hold office, nor to intermarry with white people; and I will say in addition to this that there is a physical difference between the white and black races which I believe will forever forbid the two races living together on terms of social and political equality. And inasmuch as they cannot so live . . . I as much as any other man am in favor of having the superior position assigned to the white race.

Negroes know that as the Civil War progressed Lincoln's views became more liberal, yet he never brought himself to believe that the colored man was the equal of the white man in all respects. At the end of his life he was recommending that Negroes who had fought in the Union armies, and perhaps the "very intelligent" who were not veterans, be given the vote. That was as far as he ever went. And so Lincoln comes down, at least part way, from his pedestal.

This verdict, of course, takes the Civil War President out of the context of his time. It ignores the situation of the Negro in 1865. In that year slavery was abolished, but that was the only condition of his life that changed. Most Negroes were illiterate: in bondage they had been prevented from learning to read and write. Few had skills other than those of the plantation worker. Few, at least in the South, knew anything of the world beyond the fields in which they worked. In general — of course there were many exceptions — the Negro in 1865 was not the white man's equal.

The Negro today bears little resemblance to his predecessor of a century ago except in the color of his skin. He is no longer unaware of the world, he is literate, he has proved his capability in every field of endeavor. What Lincoln said about the Negro of his time cannot, in fairness, be applied to the Negro in 1965, but if we think it will not be so applied, we delude ourselves.

This is to say that inevitably attitudes and convictions that prevail now will color appraisals of the import of a life that came to an end a hundred years ago. In short, there will certainly be reappraisals of the Lincoln legacy.

It may be instructive, in this connection, to review what a few earlier writers, choosing only those of full knowledge and high perceptiveness, have had to say about the meaning of Lincoln's life. I start with Isaac N. Arnold, Lincoln's friend of many years, his unwavering supporter in Congress, a scholar of high competence whose *Life of Abraham Lincoln* was published in 1885. To Arnold, Lincoln was above all a paragon of manhood, endowed with a tender heart, a direct and honest mind, quiet firmness, and a forgiving spirit. And what, in Arnold's opinion, did Lincoln accomplish in the four years of his administration? "He composed the bitter quarrels of rival military leaders, and at length discovered and placed at the head of his armies the skill and ability which secured military success." In addition, while keeping pace with public sentiment, "he struck blow after blow at the institution of slavery, until he proclaimed emancipation, and crowned his work by an amendment to the Constitution, prohibiting slavery throughout the republic, thus realizing the dream of his early years."

In short, Arnold saw Lincoln as an exemplary human being who preserved the Union by military perspicuity and freed the slaves.

I turn next to John G. Nicolay and John Hay, the two young men who served as Lincoln's secretaries during the war years and knew him more intimately than any other of his contemporaries. In the concluding chapter of their great biography — and it is a great book — Lincoln appears as the ideal man, a man of courage, justice, wisdom, and humanity who grew steadily to meet the enormous problems with which he was confronted.

"There are two classes of men whose names are more enduring than any monument," Nicolay and Hay wrote, "— the great writers; and the men of great achievement, the founders of states, the conquerors. Lincoln has the singular fortune to belong to both these categories; upon these broad and stable foundations his renown is securely built."

In their summation the authors made no mention of

Lincoln's advocacy of democracy or of emancipation, although both attributes are fully treated in their text.

No person did more to shape the twentieth-century conception of Lincoln than the British biographer, Lord Charnwood. To him, Lincoln's greatness lay in the fact that he had saved the Union and freed the slaves, and that he had "quite purged his heart and mind from hatred or even anger towards his fellow-countrymen." With certain qualifications his name is the greatest among those associated with the cause of popular government. "No political theory stands out from his words or actions; but they show a most unusual sense of the possible dignity of common men and common things."

My last testator will be James G. Randall himself. I quote from the concluding paragraph of his masterly article on Lincoln in the *Dictionary of American Biography,* published in 1933.

> That he [Lincoln] was among the "consummate masters of statecraft" may be disputed, but such was the impression he left that this distinction has been accorded him. In the shortest list of American liberal leaders he takes eminent place: liberalism with him was no garment; it was of the fiber of his mind. His hold upon the affections of his own people has not been due merely to the fact that he, a backwoods lad, rose to the highest office in the land. It is doubtful whether any other leader of the North could have matched him in dramatizing the war to the popular mind, in shaping language to his purposes, in smoothing personal difficulties by a magnanimous touch or a tactful gesture, in avoiding domestic and international complications, in courageously persisting in the face of almost unendurable discouragements, in maintaining war morale while

refusing to harbor personal malice against the South. Not inappropriately, he has become a symbol both of American democracy and the Union.

It is possible, I believe, to arrive at a consensus — a magic word today — from these evaluations of the significance of Lincoln's life and achievements. That consensus would embody the following points:

1. That he was a man of rare virtue.
2. That he preserved the Union.
3. That in preserving the Union he proved that democracy, as a form of government, could survive the most determined assaults that could be made upon it.
4. That he not only provided this tangible proof but also spoke in advocacy of democracy with unmatched eloquence and effectiveness.
5. That he freed the slaves.

Although I have deduced these conclusions from only four witnesses, counting Nicolay and Hay as one, I do not believe that they would be different had I drawn upon forty, or even four hundred. I predict, however, that we will find some of these judgments, or at least the significance of these judgments, challenged very soon.

No one is likely to dispute the conclusion that Lincoln was a man of rare personal virtue. But is the preservation of the Union likely to be unanimously accepted as meritorious? Before answering that question I ask you to reflect upon the fact that in the last twenty years the United States has had a part in the division of at least three nations: Germany, Korea, and Viet Nam.

Can we be quite so sure as we once were that what we took for granted is still completely valid?

And, in the light of the last few years, can we be sure that the Union really was preserved? With Confederate flags flying in several states, with such slogans as "Forget, Hell!" on the lips of many thousands, can we truly say that the country measures up to Lincoln's definition of a nation in which "the mystic chords of memory" stretch from "every battle-field and patriot grave"?

Consider democracy. In Lincoln's time the democratic form of government was definitely on trial. Monarchy prevailed in every important nation. Even in England only the upper classes had the vote. France had undergone a bloody revolution in the name of Liberty, Equality, and Fraternity, only to resolve itself into an empire in a few years. Two subsequent revolutions had not restored government to the people. Neither Germany nor Italy was even a unified state, let alone one in which popular government prevailed.

The American Civil War was hardly over before the march toward self-government and democracy began. Canada took a long step in that direction with the British North America Act of 1867. In Great Britain the Reform Bills of 1867 and 1884 extended the franchise to all classes. In France the Franco-Prussian War toppled Napoleon III and ushered in the Third Republic, and in 1875 a republican constitution was adopted. Democracy even seeped into Germany, unified in 1871, and Italy, unified in 1870; and they lived under liberal constitutions. Even Russia, darkest of the European despotisms, appeared to emerge from the shadows with the Kerensky government of 1917, while China, under the leadership of Sun Yat-sen, abolished empire and took steps in the direction of government by the people.

So, for half a century after his death, Abraham Lincoln seemed to be the harbinger and most eloquent advocate of a form of government destined to sweep the world.

What of the situation today? It is obvious that democracy has failed to sweep the world, and may not ever. Many millions in China, in Russia, and in the other nations of the communist bloc live under a class dictatorship; other millions, notably in Cuba, Spain, and Portugal, live under personal dictatorships. One would be hard put to describe the form of government which prevails in the new African nations, but few can be called democracies. What is more, there is plenty of evidence that in at least some of the nondemocratic states the people are quite content with their situation and happy with a higher standard of living, regardless of the cost in political power and individual freedom.

In view of these facts, may we not expect some challenge to Lincoln's belief in democracy and his advocacy of that form of government as a basis of his enduring fame?

Finally, I come to Lincoln the Emancipator. I happen to believe that he was the Emancipator. I have little patience with those writers who contend that he should be denied that distinction because the Proclamation of Emancipation applied only to areas where it could not, at the time, be enforced, and left slavery in the border states untouched. They ignore the fact that as the Union armies moved into the South hundreds of thousands of slaves were freed; they fail to explain how some 300,000 Negroes, most of them former slaves, got into blue uniforms; and they close their eyes to the causal connection between the Emancipation Proclamation and the Thirteenth Amendment. They also overlook Lincoln's decisive role in securing the passage of that amendment by Congress.

But I predict that there will soon be those who will be saying, in the light of the Second American Revolution, that emancipation was not enough: that in freeing the slaves Lincoln did not make them free. In fact, this is already being said. I have before me a book review (*New York Herald Tribune Book Week,* April 18, 1965) by Gwendolyn Brooks, distinguished Negro poet, in which this passage occurs:

> We remember not only the Lincoln steadiness but also the totterings and peregrinations. We remember that he did not endorse black-and-white equality in political power; that he did endorse schemes for colonial settlement of Negroes in Africa and entreated Negro leaders to cooperate, citing the "physical difference broader than exists between almost any other two races" as constituting a permanent "ban" upon Negroes; that, early, he had not been opposed to gradual or partial emancipation — despising slavery yet could he say, "If I could save the Union without freeing any slaves I would do it; and if I could save it by freeing all

the slaves I would do it; and if I could save it by freeing some and leaving others alone, I would do that."

Miss Brooks goes on to express her belief that had Lincoln lived he would have come out foursquare for equality, but there will be others who will simply let the record stand, thus reducing Lincoln's stature as a champion of human freedom.

When I suggest the probability of these new interpretations I do not mean to imply that I subscribe to them. I continue to believe that Lincoln was right in making a supreme effort to preserve the Union, not only because it was his constitutional duty to do so, but also because it was a positive good that the country remain unified. I say this in the light of my conviction that the world would be better off today if the old Austro-Hungarian state had not been fragmented, and if Germany, Korea, Viet Nam, and India had not been divided.

I am convinced that Lincoln's vision of democracy remains a valid one, not perhaps as a form of government suited to all people, but in the sense of what Lincoln saw as its ultimate objective: "to elevate the condition of men — to lift artificial weights from all shoulders — to clear the paths of laudable pursuit for all — to afford all an unfettered start and a fair chance in the race of life." And I cannot see why Lincoln should not be accorded full credit for emancipation even though that achievement was in large part nullified after his death.

In this summation of Lincoln's life, with the full record before us, there are other points that need to be made — points that are called for by the conditions of our time, and might not have been stressed even a generation ago. In a day when lapses from strict moral standards confront us everywhere — in government, in business, in society — we need the example of a man of complete integrity. Lincoln spent his life in occupations susceptible to temptation — the law and politics — yet not even a suspicion of scandal ever touched him.

Of course his integrity went far beyond financial honesty. On important questions I do not think he would have been influenced by public opinion polls. You will remember that as a member of Congress he opposed the Mexican War — and forfeited any chance he might have had for reelection. On the subject of the justice of the war he wrote to his law partner:

"You [meaning Lincoln himself] are compelled to speak, and your only alternative is to tell the truth or tell a lie." A few years later he supported the Fugitive Slave Law although he disliked it intensely. His stand made him unpopular with many Republicans. He conceded that the federal government could not interfere with slavery in the states where it existed, a position that was offensive to the abolitionist wing of his party. His first loyalty was to the Constitution, and in that loyalty he would be outspoken, no matter what the cost.

Another of Lincoln's outstanding qualities needs emphasis today. I refer to his peculiar approach to grave problems. To avoid labels reminiscent of the 1964 presidential campaign let us call it deliberateness, and define the word as the habit of weighing facts and arguments before reaching a decision.

On his first full day as President, Lincoln came face to face with a crucial problem. Major Robert Anderson, beleaguered at Fort Sumter, would soon run out of supplies. Should the garrison be evacuated, supplied, or reinforced? Peace or war would hinge on the answer to this question. Lincoln deliberated. Nothing would be lost by taking time; much might be gained. In the end, time ran out. But when the war came the South, by opening fire instead of permitting the peaceful provisioning of 120 hungry men, stood before the world as the aggressor.

The Emancipation Proclamation offers another example. As early as July, 1862, Lincoln had concluded that a proclamation of emancipation, based upon military necessity, was esssential to the cause of the Union. On the advice of his cabinet he postponed action until the North should win a major battle. In late August, in a letter to Horace Greeley, he argued the case as if he had not already made up his mind — and perhaps he had not. On September 13, in a meeting with Chicago clergymen, he advanced strong reasons against emancipation without, however, committing himself. Then, on September 17, came the battle of Antietam. Five days later Lincoln issued the preliminary proclamation. He had taken two months, perhaps much longer, for deliberation.

Finally, I come back to an element common to all appraisals of Lincoln's life: his rare virtue as a human being. I should consider this trait well enough established as not to need mention except for my belief that at a time when "arm twisting" and "head knocking" seem to be prized persuaders we need to recall that a man of magnanimity and good will could also be a great statesman. Of many examples of these qualities perhaps the best can be found in Lincoln's attitude toward the Confederates.

Throughout the war he refused to speak of "enemies," preferring the word "adversaries" or the phrase "those people over there." As the war ended, many in the North demanded punishment for those who had brought it on. But not Lincoln. There had been too much bloodshed already, and he wanted only "to bind up the nation's wounds" and "to do all which may achieve a just, and a lasting peace, among ourselves, and with all nations."

Thomas Jefferson, well aware that he had earned a secure place in history, took pains to specify what he wanted to be remembered for, and directed that on the simple stone over his grave he should be identified as the author of the Declaration of Independence and the Virginia statute for religious freedom, and as the father of the University of Virginia. Abraham Lincoln, all unknowingly, wrote an even more moving epitaph. It is to be found in his response to a serenade a few days after the presidential election of 1864. "So long as I have been here," he said, "I have not willingly planted a thorn in any man's bosom."

Poems of the Civil War

BY MARK VAN DOREN

I am not going to discourse upon the poetry of the Civil War, for it is too vast a subject to be treated from the outside. I am going to try to get inside of it; I shall present and discuss a few poems which the Civil War produced. It might be easier to pretend to know the history of this vast subject, but of course no one does.

What shall we say about the poetry of the Civil War except this, that the greatest poet of the war was Abraham Lincoln? There is no question in my mind at all that this is true. His life was a poem; and I am not using the word sentimentally, I hope. His life was real as only a poem can be. And his utterances, even though they took the form of prose, cannot deceive us: they are poetry. The distinction between prose and verse is clear and mechanical; the distinction between prose and poetry is harder to make, more profound, more important. Poetry may be found either in prose or in verse. I think we all know that the Gettysburg speech is a poem; it is nonsense to call it anything else. We know the Second Inaugural is; we know the Farewell Address to the people of Springfield is. We know that the prose of Lincoln, by and large, is poetry. His letters, his memorandums, anything he wrote was the work, for me, of a great and deep and serious poet.

His only intention when he wrote was to make himself clear. That may seem very little to say for anyone, but remember how few people are clear. Remember how hard it is to be clear. Remember how many of us complain chronically because we are misunderstood. We are misunderstood only because we do not make ourselves clear. Lincoln hoped to do that. His effort, his straining effort, in most of his utterances is to make himself clear beyond the possibility of misunderstanding. That is why he read Euclid when he traveled on the circuit. The book he took with him to read over the weekends was a book of geometry. When the other lawyers asked him why he read that book he said: "I am trying to find out what it means to demonstrate something."

His handwriting, which we can see all over Springfield in facsimiles, is clear. He didn't want any word to be mistaken, and no word ever has been mistaken. It was clear from the beginning. This passion for clarity is almost unique among human beings. Most people don't care that much to be clear. Many people, perhaps, don't have that much to be clear about. In his case there was much to be clear about, and this passion to be clear —well, there is no greater virtue. The Romans of the old days had a word which they reserved for the final praise of any man. It was CLARUS, clear. It seems to have meant more than we often mean by clear. It meant everything good and great and profound and worthy.

In such a perspective Lincoln is the great poet of the Civil War. Yet he has rivals. Walt Whitman is a rival. It can be claimed that Whitman was the great poet of that war. Coming closer to our own time, we can claim that Carl Sandburg too is a great poet of that same war, although his great poem also is in prose — *Abraham Lincoln: The War Years.* I would say that Allan Nevins' work proceeding now, *The Ordeal of the Union,* hopefully to be ten volumes at least, is a historical work of truly epic proportions; and epic is a poetic word. I use the word seriously; I call Mr. Nevins a poet and I hope he doesn't mind. I would call Bruce Catton a poet if he were here. Are his books not epics? Are the sections of that narrative he has been writing of the war not the cantos of an epic poem? I think so. That is the way they affect me. And I could go on.

Maybe I should have started by saying that the

poetry of the Civil War is at its most charming in its songs. The number of songs that we can associate with the Civil War is immense. Of course we all know "Glory Hallelujah," or "John Brown's Body," though we may not know the name of its author, Charles Sprague Hall. The "Battle Hymn of the Republic" we do all know to be by Julia Ward Howe. We may not remember that the "Battle Cry of Freedom" was by George Frederick Root, and "Tenting on the Old Camp Ground" by Walter Kittredge. "Marching Through Georgia" we are more likely to remember was written by Henry Clay Work. "Three Hundred Thousand More" was by James Sloan Gibbons. Possibly it is these songs, and thousands more like them, maybe better, maybe worse, that ultimately are the poetry of the Civil War, because there is nothing more important than song.

In the South too there were songs. I don't need to remind you of "Dixie," which we know in two versions, an old one and a younger one. The old one was by Daniel D. Emmett, the younger one by Albert Pike. Then there was "My Maryland" by James Ryder Randall, and "The Bonnie Blue Flag," by Annie Chambers Ketchum. You probably remember, speaking of "Dixie," how when Lee had surrendered at Appomattox and there was a crowd on the White House lawn asking Mr. Lincoln to come out and speak to them, he did go out and after a few words turned to the band and said: "I now want you, as a special favor to me, to play a song that I have always liked but which only recently has been captured at Appomattox." That song was "Dixie."

The war itself, however, sometimes seems to me to be a poem, and would be even if no one had ever written about it. Now that is probably nonsense. Yet this particular war was a great and wonderful and terrible and beautiful thing, and so is a kind of poem. And out of itself it produced poems of magnitude as well as the songs of which I have spoken. I have already spoken of Carl Sandburg's *The War Years,* many of whose critics don't realize it is a poem. Stephen Vincent Benet's "John Brown's Body," is of course in verse, and as such it is the nearest approach to an epic about the Civil War that we have and I admire it very much; but I would not for a minute expect it to remain even in the balance with Sandburg's *Lincoln.* I mean the balance of poetry.

I don't need to remind you, perhaps, of all the poets of that time who wrote short verses about the war. Some of you may not know how deeply interested Herman Melville was in it. He had finished his great work in fiction almost ten years before the war began. It moved him very deeply and again and again he touched upon it as he did in his poem "Shiloh." John Greenleaf Whittier and Henry Wadsworth Longfellow kept busy with the subject too. I don't need to remind you of Whittier's "Barbara Frietchie," Longfellow's "The Cumberland," and the tragic sinking of that vessel at Hampton Roads. Not everybody, I find, knows even the name of Henry Howard Brownell, a poet whose war lyrics, published in 1866 as a volume, make one of the most distinguished collections we have had. I have never quite understood why he has not become better known. He might be known only for his magnificent poem about the review of the grand army in Washington when the war was over. We have all read accounts of how regiment after regiment, division after division, army after army marched down the streets of Washington with bands playing and all sorts of dignitaries reviewing them from stands. I don't know that anyone more eloquently than Brownell refers to the one man who wasn't there; to the one man who should have been there; to the one man who had made those armies, who had mastered their masters, whose will and whose imagination had fashioned that war in the way it went: Lincoln himself. Brownell represents him as being there nevertheless: a great invisible ghost seated high above all the other dignitaries watching those armies that he had brooded and worried and agonized over so much.

And of course, in addition to the great long poem of Walt Whitman there were all the little ones that he wrote during the war, and at the end of it published in a volume called *Drum-Taps*. I don't know how many people read *Drum-Taps*. I suppose a great many people do. I hope you do, I hope everyone has. I would like to present just one of those short poems. Later I shall include part of the long poem, but this is a good example of the short ones.

Come up from the fields father, here's a letter from our
Pete,
And come to the front door mother, here's a letter from thy
dear son.

Lo, 'tis autumn,
Lo, were the trees, deeper green, yellower and redder,

Cool and sweeten Ohio's villages with leaves fluttering in the moderate wind,
Where apples ripe in the orchards hang and grapes on the trellis'd vines,
(Smell you the smell of the grapes on the vines?
Smell you the buckwheat where the bees were lately buzzing?)

Above all, lo, the sky so calm, so transparent after the rain, and with wondrous clouds,
Below too, all calm, all vital and beautiful, and the farm prospers well.

Down in the fields all prospers well,
But now from the fields come father, come at the daughter's call,
And come to the entry mother, to the front door come right away.

Fast as she can she hurries, something ominous, her steps trembling,
She does not tarry to smooth her hair nor adjust her cap.

Open the envelope quickly,
O this is not our son's writing, yet his name is sign'd,
O a strange hand writes for our dear son, O stricken mother's soul!
All swims before her eyes, flashes with black, she catches the main words only,
Sentences broken, *gunshot wound in the breast, cavalry skirmish, taken to hospital,*
At present low, but will soon be better.

Ah now the single figure to me,
Amid all teeming and wealthy Ohio with all its cities and farms,
Sickly white in the face and dull in the head, very faint,
By the jamb of a door leans.

Grieve not so, dear mother, (the just-grown daughter speaks
through her sobs,
The little sisters huddle around speechless and dismay'd,)
See, dearest mother, the letter says Pete will soon be better.

Alas poor boy, he will never be better, (not may-be needs
to be better, that brave and simple soul,)
While they stand at home at the door he is dead already,
The only son is dead.
But the mother needs to be better,
She with thin form presently drest in black,
By day her meals untouch'd, then at night fitfully sleeping,
often waking,
In the midnight walking, weeping, longing with one deep
longing,
O that she might withdraw unnoticed, silent from life
escape and withdraw,
To follow, to seek, to be with her dear dead son.

The dead of the Civil War — nearly a million men died of wounds and disease — have been the subject, naturally, of many poets, either individually as in this case or in the mass. There has never been any end to the contemplation of the young men and the old men who died during those four years. In the North, for example, there was Theodore O'Hara's "The Bivouac of the Dead"; almost anyone sooner or later encounters that.

Some 30 years ago, if you will forgive me for including one of my own poems, I was all but obsessed, as many people have been, by the spectacle of the countless boys who did not come back from the war. We write histories of wars without adequate recognition, it seems to me, of the men who died in them. Of course we speak of them, and annually we celebrate them — I know that — but the historian tends to have as his subject those who survived. We talk about how the country was later: whether it was better or worse. Perhaps we don't know what to say about those who gave up their lives. Well, once I was so absorbed in this question that I saw somehow an imaginary region of the United States in which all the boys of the North and the South, half buried in the sod, wanted to come back and yet were unable to. The poem is called simply "Civil War":

The country is no country I have seen,
And no man goes there who is now alive, and no man
Ever is going to leave there. But they try —
Waving a million beards that on pale faces
Blacken with time and spread.
It is a field of bodies of blue boys,
And gray boys, grown half way into the ground.
The wind is dark that sways them —
All of them bending with it, south or north,
All of them straining here; but no one knowing
Of any fellow by who gazes too.
It is a field of legless bearded boys
With bright unnecessary buttons on their breasts,
And skirts of coats that hold them in the sod.
The bodies twist,
The circular, small eyes are mad with being;
A million mouths fly open without sound;
But none can tear his coat up, that must come
With roots and worms or come not up at all.

Away in Carolina, Maine, Wisconsin,
Boys who kept their legs walked long and long.
They set their feet in furrows, or in aisles;
They strolled with girls, were taken, and were fathers;

Had old companionship, and last were covered
Quietly with smooth boards, and grass, and stone.
Stiffly now they hold society;
Forever this they lie without a want.

In the forbidden country where the sod
Grows down and down, with blue roots, gray roots,
In the dark windy land no one can leave,
Separate necks yearn homeward;
Separate hungry shoulders pull and pull.
Wind, oh wind, I did not come to stay;
I must be there tomorrow, not to miss —
But the dark wind is earless, and the day
Is endless, and the grasses hiss and hiss.[1]

One thing we know about any soldier in any war is that he did not want to be where he was. He wanted to be home, and counted on being there tomorrow or next month or next year. Perhaps the most serious thought we can have about a war is about all those who thought they would come home — had maybe very important things to do there — yet never did. Their lives, if they had been continued, might have made a difference which historians would have to take account of. But the historians, of course, cannot take account of it. That is where poetry comes in.

The dead of the South have been celebrated also by Henry Timrod of South Carolina in his very fine poem "Magnolia Cemetery," sung at Charleston in 1867, and in our own time by Allen Tate in his famous poem "Ode to the Confederate Dead," of which I can give you only a sample with apologies to him. It is a very mov-

[1] Mark Van Doren, "Civil War" in *Now the Sky and Other Poems* (New York: Charles and Albert Boni, 1928).

ing, eloquent poem which no reader of it has ever forgotten.

Row after row with strict impunity
The headstones yield their names to the elements,
The wind whirrs without recollection;
In the riven troughs the splayed leaves
Pile up, of nature the casual sacrament
To the seasonal eternity of death;
Then driven by the fierce scrutiny
Of heaven to their election in the vast breath,
They sough the rumour of mortality.

Autumn is desolation in the plot
Of a thousand acres where these memories grow
From the inexhaustible bodies that are not
Dead, but feed the grass row after rich row.
Think of the autumns that have come and gone! —
Ambitious November with the humors of the year,
With a particular zeal for every slab,
Staining the uncomfortable angels that rot
On the slabs, a wing chipped here, an arm there:
The brute curiosity of an angel's stare
Turns you, like them, to stone,
Transforms the heaving air
Till plunged to a heavier world below
You shift your sea-space blindly
Heaving, turning like the blind crab.

Dazed by the wind, only the wind
The leaves flying, plunge. . . .[2]

Now Mr. Lincoln was not only the great poet of the war; he was the subject of its greatest poetry. There can be no question about that. I wonder how many know

[2] Allen Tate, "Ode to the Confederate Dead," in *Selected Poems by Allen Tate* (New York: Charles Scribner's Sons, 1937).

a poem that Edwin Arlington Robinson wrote about Lincoln rather early in his own career. He published it with a note saying: "Supposed to have been written not long after the Civil War." It refers to the important fact that almost everybody in Lincoln's time made fun of him. We take Lincoln seriously, but he was seldom taken seriously then. The majority of persons laughed at him, at least a little bit. Many Americans, even to the end, were ashamed of him. He didn't look like a President, and he had roused a fury of dissent which again was most disturbing. There were those who worshipped him, I know, but the calm that surrounds the name, the image of Lincoln that now is felt in almost all the bronzes we have of him — that calm came only after his death. Robinson's poem "The Master" is about those who ridiculed Lincoln while he lived; the speaker, indeed, is one of those who had. Below is the first stanza of it, and then a little more.

A flying word from here and there
Had sown the name at which we sneered,
But soon the name was everywhere,
To be reviled and then revered:
A presence to be loved and feared,
We cannot hide it, or deny
That we, the gentlemen who jeered,
May be forgotten by and by.

. . . .

The face we see was never young
Nor could it wholly have been old.

For he, to whom we had applied
Our shopman's test of age and worth,

Was elemental when he died,
As he was ancient at his birth:
The saddest among kings of earth,
Bowed with a galling crown, this man
Met rancor with a cryptic mirth,
Laconic — and Olympian.[3]

That reminds me of one of my favorite passages in the works of Lincoln. You may or may not know that in 1863 a Shakespearian actor went to Washington playing in "Hamlet" and "Macbeth," and Lincoln wrote him a letter praising his acting and praising the plays. We now know that Lincoln knew Shakespeare as he knew the Bible. They were his books. His education came from Shakespeare and the Bible and Euclid — together with some law books, too, but I don't remember which ones they were. His letter is a distinguished piece of Shakespearian criticism; but James H. Hackett, the actor — who had the vanity of many actors — showed it to everybody he saw and it finally fell into the hands of some newspapermen and was published. Then the jeering was all but national at this President who considered himself a dramatic critic. He had made a fool of himself in many ways, but now he was making a fool of himself by going to the theater, by being interested in Shakespeare, and by writing to an actor. Hackett was ashamed of what he had done and wrote to Lincoln to say so. This is the answer he got:

Give yourself no uneasiness on the subject. . . . My note to you I certainly did not expect to see in print; yet I have

[3] Edwin Arlington Robinson, "The Master," in *The Town down the River* (New York: Charles Scribner's Sons, 1910).

not been much shocked by the newspaper comments upon it. Those comments constitute a fair specimen of what has occurred to me through life. I have endured a great deal of ridicule without much malice; and have received a great deal of kindness, not quite free from ridicule. I am used to it.

I give you that as a sentence from one of the greatest writers who ever used the English language. It is so good that you won't be able to remember it. You will try to say it and you will get it wrong. I will repeat it at least once more. I myself cannot remember it. I haven't got the brains. This is the merciless, relentless logic of which I have spoken; this is the man who always had to be clear.

I have endured a great deal of ridicule without much malice; and have received a great deal of kindness, not quite free from ridicule.

Here is Lincoln himself saying he is aware that he has been an object of ridicule; yet he has known how to get used to it and even to triumph over the fact.

I also wish to mention several poems that have been written about Lincoln in the time since his death, indeed in our own time, in our own century; poems that represent him as somehow still available to us. Gwendolyn Brooks, in the fine poem of hers "In the Time of Detachment, in the Time of Cold," spoke mainly of the goodness which keeps him alive in our minds. This has happened over and over again. We cannot forget Mr. Lincoln. We bring him back; we want him about us in times of trouble. Those of you who were at the White House on Lincoln's birthday this year were impressed, I know, by President Johnson's saying in a little speech he made that often at night, when he could not sleep because he wasn't sure what he should do the next day, he heard Lincoln walking in the halls. I asked him later whether he ever heard any other President walking there. No, he said, Lincoln was the only one. Again Lincoln had come back. He came back in the poem that I am sure you all know by Vachel Lindsay, a poem written during World War I, "Abraham Lincoln Walks at Midnight." Perhaps I don't need to include this poem — you must know it — yet here it is.

It is portentous, and a thing of state
That here at midnight, in our little town
A mourning figure walks, and will not rest,
Near the old court-house pacing up and down,

Or by his homestead, or in shadowed yards
He lingers where his children used to play,
Or through the market, on the well-worn stones
He stalks until the dawn-stars burn away.

A bronzed, lank man! His suit of ancient black,
A famous high top-hat and plain worn shawl
Make him the quaint great figure that men love,
The prairie-lawyer, master of us all.

He cannot sleep upon his hillside now.
He is among us: — as in times before!
And we who toss and lie awake for long
Breathe deep, and start, to see him pass the door.

His head is bowed. He thinks on men and kings.
Yea, when the sick world cries, how can he sleep?
Too many peasants fight, they know not why,
Too many homesteads in black terror weep.

The sins of all the war-lords burn his heart.
He sees the dreadnaughts scouring every main.
He carries on his shawl-wrapped shoulders now
The bitterness, the folly and the pain.

He cannot rest until a spirit-dawn
Shall come; — the shining hope of Europe free:
The league of sober folk, the Workers' Earth,
Bringing a long peace to Cornland, Alp and Sea.

It breaks his heart that kings must murder still,
That all his hours of travail here for men
Seem yet in vain. And who will bring white peace
That he may sleep upon his hill again?[4]

Not all of you may know the poem that John Gould Fletcher wrote saying much the same sort of thing a few years later, between the two great world wars which we have had the sadness to witness. Fletcher was a man from Arkansas. I knew him well, and always thought of him as an absolutely unreconstructed southerner. I have always been astonished by his poem called "Lincoln." It moves me not only because of its own merit but because Fletcher wrote it. A southerner wrote it — we must remember that, particularly in the last few lines.

Like a gaunt, scraggly pine
Which lifts its head above the mournful sandhills;
And patiently, through dull years of bitter silence,
Untended and uncared for, starts to grow.

Ungainly, laboring, huge,
The wind of the north has twisted and gnarled its branches;

[4] Vachel Lindsay, "Abraham Lincoln Walks at Midnight," in *The Congo and Other Poems* (New York: Macmillan Co., 1914). Copyright renewed 1942 by Elizabeth C. Lindsay.

Yet in the heat of mid-summer days, when thunder clouds ring the horizon,
A nation of men shall rest beneath its shade.

And it shall protect them all,
Hold everyone safe there, watching aloof in silence;
Until at last, one mad stray bolt from the zenith
Shall strike it in an instant down to earth.

There was a darkness in this man, an immense and hollow darkness,
Of which we may not speak, nor share with him nor enter;
A darkness through which strong roots stretched downwards into the earth
Towards old things;

Towards the herdsman-kings who walked the earth and spoke with God,
Towards the wanderers who sought for they knew not what and found their goal at last;
Towards the men who waited, only waited patiently when all seemed lost,
Many bitter winters of defeat;

Down to the granite of patience,
These roots swept, knotted fibrous roots, prying, piercing, seeking,
And drew from the living rock and the living waters about it,
The red sap to carry upwards to the sun.

Not proud, but humble,
Only to serve and pass on, to endure to the end through service,
For the axe is laid at the roots of the trees, and all that bring not forth good fruit
Shall be cut down on the day to come and cast into the fire.

There is a silence abroad in the land to-day,

And in the hearts of men, a deep and anxious silence;
And, because we are still at last, those bronze lips slowly open,
Those hollow and weary eyes take on a gleam of light.

Slowly a patient, firm-syllabled voice cuts through the endless silence,
Like laboring oxen that drag a plough through the chaos of rude clay-fields.

Then here are the final lines of which I have spoken:

Over the uproar of cities,
Over the million intricate threads of life wavering and crossing,
In the midst of problems we know not, tangling, perplexing, ensnaring,
Rises one white tomb along.

Beam over it, stars,
Wrap it 'round, stripes — stripes red for the pain that he bore for you —
Enfold it forever, O flag, rent, soiled, but repaired through your anguish;
Long as you keep him there safe, the nations shall bow to your law.

Strew over him flowers:
Blue forget-me-nots from the north and the bright pink arbutus
From the east, and from the west rich orange blossom,
But from the heart of the land take the passion-flower;

Rayed, violet, dim,
With the nails that pierced, the cross that he bore and the circlet,

And beside it there lay also one lonely snow-white magnolia,
Bitter for remembrance of the healing which has past.[5]

The number of these distinguished and beautiful poems is very great: poems in which Lincoln has been as it were summoned from his tomb when he was needed. Carl Sandburg wrote such a poem in 1944. It is called "The Long Shadow of Lincoln," and it begins with a quotation from the great address of Lincoln to Congress on December 1, 1862: "We can succeed only by concert. . . . The dogmas of the quiet past are inadequate to the stormy present. The occasion is piled high with difficulty, and we must rise with the occasion. As our case is new, so we must think anew and act anew. We must disenthrall ourselves." Carl Sandburg says:

Be sad, be cool, be kind,
Remembering those now dream-dust
Hallowed in the ruts and gullies,
Solemn bones under the smooth blue sea,
Faces war-blown in a falling rain.

Be a brother, if so can be,
To those beyond battle fatigue
Each in his own corner of earth
Or forty fathoms undersea
Beyond all boom of guns,
Beyond any bong of a great bell,
Each with a bosom and number,
Each with a pack of secrets,
Each with a personal dream and doorway,
And over them now the long endless winds

[5] John Gould Fletcher, "Lincoln," in *Selected Poems* (New York: Farrar & Rinehart, 1938). Copyright 1938 by John Gould Fletcher, renewed 1966 by Charlie May Fletcher.

With the low healing song of time.
The hush and sleep and murmur of time.
Make your wit a guard and cover.
Sing low, sing high, sing wide.
Let your laughter come free
Remembering looking toward peace:
"We must disenthrall ourselves."

At the end once more he asks for laughter, as if Lincoln would like that too.

There is dust alive.
Out of a granite tomb,
Out of a bronze sarcophagus,
Loose from the stone and copper
Steps of white-smoke ghost,
Lifting an authoritative hand
In the name of dreams worth dying for,
In the name of men whose dust breathes
Of those dreams so worth dying for;
What they did being past words,
Beyond all smooth and easy telling.[6]

The thing I remember most vividly out of Lloyd Lewis' great book *Myths After Lincoln* is his account of the typical man who daily visits the tomb of Lincoln, looks at that great marble block that holds him down, and says: "He isn't there." Such a man is not referring to the fact that some counterfeiters once planned to steal the body; that isn't it. He means that Lincoln never was mere flesh. He always was somehow risen. He cannot be buried, he cannot be kept down. And that is what our dear friend Carl is trying to say. He knows

[6] Carl Sandburg, "The Long Shadow of Lincoln: A Litany," in *Saturday Evening Post,* Vol. CCXVII, No. 33 (February 10, 1945).

about the weight of cement which is over that body now, yet out of it like a white smoke ghost Lincoln rises and is available to us.

I must move on to my conclusion. I spoke of the great long poem that Whitman wrote concerning Lincoln. Everyone knows that his masterpiece was "When Lilacs Last in the Dooryard Bloom'd" and everyone knows that it is the master poem which Lincoln inspired. It is too long to include here and I don't need to include it. I can merely say that if you have not read it you should do so at the first opportunity because it is one of the great poems in our language, with its interweaving of the images of the sprig of lilac, the evening star, the cloud, Whitman's own thought about the man who had died, and the song of the bird which he heard singing in the swamp and which told him how to understand the death of that man. For in April, 1865, Whitman, like so many persons then and like so many persons in November, 1963, felt utterly helpless in the face of a death that had occurred. They didn't know what to do about it; they didn't know what to say about it. They certainly didn't know what to think about it. They were surrounded by nothing but darkness. Whitman represents himself as going through this agony, and of being saved from it by the memory of a sprig of lilac that he had picked that April, by the memory of the evening star that was sinking when he heard the bird, and particularly by his memory of a mockingbird he had overheard. A bird whose song told him that all that had happened was that a man had died, that death had once more come into the world. Death in this poem becomes a vast and beautiful thing. It is Whitman's distinction, as it is the distinction of any great poet, that he somehow conquers the subject of death, ceases to be afraid of it, finds it ultimately beautiful. The heart of the poem is his carol to death. We are to imagine a bird singing this.

Come lovely and soothing death,
Undulate around the world, serenely arriving, arriving,
In the day, in the night, to all, to each,
Sooner or later delicate death.

Prais'd be the fathomless universe,
For life and joy, and for objects and knowledge curious,
And for love, sweet love — but praise! praise! praise!
For the sure-enwinding arms of cool-enfolding death.

Dark mother always gliding near with soft feet,
Have none chanted for thee a chant of fullest welcome?
Then I chant it for thee, I glorify thee above all,
I bring thee a song that when thou must indeed come, come unfalteringly.

Approach strong deliveress,
When it is so, when thou hast taken them I joyously sing the dead,
Lost in the loving floating ocean of thee,
Laved in the flood of thy bliss O death.

From me to the glad serenades,
Dances for thee I propose saluting thee, adornments and feastings for thee,
And the sights of the open landscape and the high-spread sky are fitting,
And life and the fields, and the huge and thoughtful night.

The night in silence under many a star,

The ocean shore and the husky whispering wave whose voice I know,
And the soul turning to thee O vast and well-veil'd death,
And the body gratefully nestling close to thee.

Over the tree-tops I float thee a song,
Over the rising and sinking waves, over the myriad fields and the prairies wide,
Over the dense-pack'd cities all and the teeming wharves and ways,
I float this carol with joy, with joy to thee O death.

This was Whitman's way of saying that he had been saved from the awful, the unspeakable moment which followed Lincoln's assassination. He was saved by realizing that somehow or other he might conquer death, might bring it into the circle of beautiful things where of course it belongs. Maybe the death of Lincoln is like very few other deaths in that it is susceptible of such treatment, but maybe that sort of thing is what I had in mind when I began. The death of Lincoln was a poem; or if it was not one already, Whitman made it so.

The war being ended, Whitman wrote a short poem called "Reconciliation." All bitterness, all enmity, is represented in it as having gone out of the American world. The poem moves me deeply:

Word over all, beautiful as the sky,
Beautiful that war and all its deeds of carnage must in time be utterly lost,
That the hands of the sisters Death and Night incessantly softly wash again, and ever again, this soil'd world;
For my enemy is dead, a man divine as myself is dead,
I look where he lies white-faced and still in the coffin — I draw near,

Bend down and touch lightly with my lips the white face in
the coffin.

The same thing emerges in another famous poem. It is the epitaph that Edgar Lee Masters wrote for Anne Rutledge in the *Spoon River Anthology.* I read it now, in spite of the fact that Masters repudiated it; he had turned against Lincoln, and written one of the bitterest books against him ever written. However that may be, he wrote a masterpiece which I am sure will outlast almost anything else he wrote, and will outlast any final conclusions he came to about the man.

Out of me unworthy and unknown
The vibrations of deathless music:
"With malice toward none, with charity for all."
Out of me the forgiveness of millions toward millions,
And the beneficent face of a nation
Shining with justice and truth.
I am Anne Rutledge who sleep beneath these weeds,
Beloved in life of Abraham Lincoln,
Wedded to him, not through union,
But through separation.
Bloom forever, O Republic,
From the dust of my bosom![7]

[7] Edgar Lee Masters, "Anne Rutledge," in *Spoon River Anthology* (New York: Macmillan Co., 1915). Copyright 1942 by Edgar Lee Masters.

The European Reaction to Lincoln

BY SENATOR PAUL H. DOUGLAS

It is a source of inspiration to stand in the hollow of this hillside where Abraham Lincoln grew to intellectual and moral maturity, and it is with humility that one prepares his own poor offering to appear in company with those of so many close students of Lincoln and of the Civil War.

It is always a source of wonder to contrast the beginnings of Lincoln's political life here on this frontier hillside with his four years in Washington a third of a century later and with his final apotheosis there in marble. It is a still greater contrast to compare these primitive origins with the present acknowledgment by the world that he has become one of its great heroes of all time. He has become honored as the defender of the poor and the oppressed, both black and white; as the leader of great armies; and as a war leader who never uttered a word of bitterness about his antagonists. He is acclaimed as the skilled diplomat in carpet slippers, the unschooled yet self-taught rustic who, inspired by Jack Kelso perhaps in this very hollow, became one of the great masters of English prose. His Gettysburg Address is ranked with Pericles' funeral oration as one of the two finest speeches of all time and the haunting music of his letter to Mrs. Bixby and of his Second Inaugural stirs the deepest of thoughts and emotions of men and women everywhere.

Many erroneously believe that this recognition, which is now virtually worldwide, was more or less instantaneous and universal during his presidency; that the world quickly recognized him for what he was and that his course to fame was immediate and direct. It is a natural tendency for this generation to picture their grandfathers, great-grandfathers, and great-great-grandfathers as having been Lincoln's true-blue supporters and to say, "If I had lived then, I would also have been by his side." Perhaps so, but it is sobering to reflect that both in 1860 and 1864 Lincoln failed to carry Sangamon County against Stephen A. Douglas and George B. McClellan and that the majority against him was even greater in 1864 than it had been in 1860. And it is also sobering to realize that not a single minister in Sangamon County in 1860 supported Lincoln for the presidency, and I believe only a handful did so in 1864.

As it was in Sangamon County, so it was in Europe. Nearly everybody who was anybody was bitterly opposed to Lincoln and to the North. They reviled him both publicly and privately, prayed and worked for his defeat, and only repented after his death. In England the court, the nobility, the wealthy, and even the upper-middle classes were contemptuous of Lincoln. This was almost universally true of the Tory Party which represented the landowning feudal nobility and had run the country. But it was also true of the main body of the Whig Party, which had not yet formally become the Liberal Party. Witness the attitudes of the three great leaders of the Whig party at that time. Lord Palmerston, the Prime Minister, and his opposite number, with whom he alternated as Prime Minister and Foreign Minister, Lord John Russell (who was the grandfather of Bertrand Russell), were both staunch supporters of the South. The third member of the leading triumvirate in the Whig party, William E. Gladstone, was then in the process of making his painful transition from the right of the Tory party to the left of the Liberal party, but at this time he was a very strong southern sympathizer. So indeed were the clergy and virtually all the members of the established church. The journals and papers of Great Britain almost without exception were bitterly anti-Lincoln and anti-North. Every day the *Times,* under the editorship of the thundering Delany, had editorials denouncing the North and Lincoln and slanted its news columns in favor of the South. *Punch,* the weekly comic paper of the upper classes, was savage in its satirization of Lincoln. Sir John Tenniel, the greatest cartoonist of his time, loved to represent Lincoln as a bearded baboon emerging dripping from the swamps of Illinois.

It was the same in Paris where the tinseled splendor of the court of Napoleon III cast its false glitter over the life of that capital. The French leaders and the aristocracy were almost without exception pro-South. The consort of Napoleon III, the Empress Eugénie, uttered the wisecrack that there was no need for the contemporary traveler, geographer, and anthropologist Paul du Chaillu to search for the missing link between man and monkeys in Africa when by going to Washington he could find him in the person of Abraham Lincoln.

It was the same in Austria which was then still a real power on the continent, and it was the same in Belgium, whose King Leopold was a close advisor of Queen Victoria and exercised great influence upon her. Curiously enough, the only place where there was any real sympathy for Lincoln and the North among the ruling classes of Europe was in its most retarded country — Russia. Alexander II was, at the moment, sympathetic to reform and was in the process of first conceiving and then executing the emancipation of the serfs. The Russian friendship for Lincoln and the North during the war was not only a verbal one, but was manifested by detachments of their navy which appeared off both the

Pacific and the Atlantic coasts of North America to demonstrate their sympathy.

Now why did the ruling classes almost without exception oppose and satirize Lincoln and the North so bitterly? They were engaged in a death struggle inside their nations with the democratic forces which were emerging as the result of the industrial revolution, involving the creation of a wage-earning class and the movement of population from the countryside to the cities. The aristocracies did not want democracy to triumph in their own countries, and they did not want to have it triumph in the United States because they believed that it would set a bad example to the people of their nations. They prided themselves on being wellborn and believed that they were the only groups which were fit to govern. Their ancestors, by occupying and owning the land and other property, had been able to live very comfortably without performing manual labor. They believed that they had been made fit to govern by leisure and by education. That a man who had been a rail-splitter, bargeman, surveyor, and farm laborer in a rough world should be allowed to rise to high office and to perform the duties of statesman was to them abhorrent. An English nobleman, Lord Beresford-Hope, satirized Lincoln because he had filled these occupations in early life and remarked that he was not fit to be even a county judge in England.

If there was a sentimental repugnance to Lincoln and the North on the part of the ruling groups in Europe, there was also a sentimental attraction to the plantation owners of the South, for the lords of the lash also lived comfortably without doing manual labor. They had good manners toward those to whom they wished to exhibit good manners, and they lived by the code of what is said to have been the standard of British gentlemen, namely of never doing an unkind thing unintentionally. The European aristocracy therefore felt a close communion between their class and the slave owners. They believed that the slave owners were more numerous and more important than they actually were. They had not read Frederick Law Olmstead's *A Journey in the Seaboard Slave States,* but they had a sympathy for those who were booted and spurred and who intended to ride the masses of mankind who were bridled and saddled.

But there were economic as well as sentimental and emotional motives. As long as the war continued and the northern blockade was effective, the exportation of cotton from the South to Europe and particularly to England was shut off. This meant that the English textile industry of Lancashire and Yorkshire either had to greatly reduce its operations or close down completely, because England depended on American cotton. It was this simple fact which had caused South Carolina Senator James Henry Hammond to refer to cotton as king because he believed that the absence of cotton would cause Europe to take the side of the South and to oppose the North. If the war was prolonged, the exportation of cotton would be shut off by the northern naval blockade, and if the North were victorious, Britain believed production and hence its supplies would fall.

But if the South were to be victorious, and victorious fairly quickly, then cotton could move overseas, the spindles and looms of northern England would operate, business would prosper, and British finances would improve. This was the argument which won over the industrial classes in the north of Britain which had earlier opposed the Tories in the period prior to the Reform Bill of 1833 and in the struggle over the Corn Laws.

Finally, of course, there were nationalistic jealousies which made the power structure of the European countries opposed to American success. The leaders in Great Britain were still bitterly resentful of the fact that the United States had succeeded in throwing off the political control of Great Britain in the War of Independence. They did not want the United States to succeed because it might give similar ideas to the other colonies which had not yet even become dominions, let alone commonwealths. They wanted the United States to split into a series of separate governments so that the British could point to the great mistake which had been made by the Americans of the eighteenth century in throwing off the protective arm of Great Britain. Moreover, they believed that a strong America would diminish the relative power of Europe. In all this, they considered, as most power mechanics do, relative strength and relative prosperity, not absolute strength or absolute prosperity. Like the mercantilists, they could not conceive of a world in which all could be prosperous, in which there might be degrees of prosperity but in which the prosperity of one increased the prosperity of others. They believed that power and prosperity were relative and that as the United States rose so Great Britain must fall. On the continent of Europe, France and Austria took advantage of the Civil War in 1863 to set on the throne of Mexico Maximilian, an Austrian archduke and the brother of the young Emperor Francis Joseph. They wanted to have Mexico under monarchical rule as a counterpoise to the United States. They wanted to spread the principle of monarchism throughout Central America as well as in Mexico. There was probably also some negotiation with the South about a possible introdution of the monarchical system into the slave states.

So all these forces made the rulers of government and of public opinion opposed to the North and bitterly critical and contemptuous of Abraham Lincoln.

II

How did the nobility and the governing classes of these countries intend to help the South and injure the North? First they sought to do so by outfitting and equipping the Confederate Navy with ships to prey upon Union commerce. The pro-British historians have tried to pretend that Lord Russell and Lord Palmerston did not know that the *Alabama* was being built in English shipyards for precisely this purpose. As I remember, Henry Adams, who was a clerk for his father Charles Francis Adams, the American minister to Great Britain, thought that at least one of these men was innocent. This was ridiculous. Of course the Prime Minister and the Foreign Minister knew why the *Alabama* was being built. They not only knew its purpose but they protected the ship and allowed it to go to sea. This was all proved at the Geneva tribunal ten years later when a judgment against Great Britain was handed down by an international court.

Second, they wanted to help, so far as was possible, the South to float loans in both Great Britain and France and thus to furnish the Confederacy with those sinews of war which could be used directly and indirectly to provide munitions and supplies. The securing of such loans was one of the missions of James Murray Mason and John Slidell, the commissioners of the Confederate States to Great Britain and France.

Third, and perhaps most important of all, was the effort to have Great Britain, France, and other powers recognize the South as a separate nation. If they would do so, as Gladstone virtually declared Britain would, they could then claim the right to send their ships to southern ports to bring in supplies and to take out cotton. The British Navy and Merchant Marine could then have been used to break the blockade so as to get cotton flowing from the South to the factories of England. Such action would, in all probability, have involved war with the North, because the North could not have permitted this and would naturally have tried to make the blockade effective against British ships. Great Britain was on the point, I believe, of recognizing the South in the late summer of 1862. They were on the verge of doing this up until Antietam or, as the southerners say, Sharpsburg. For the first year and a half the war had been overwhelmingly favorable to the South. Bull Run had been followed the next spring by the defeat of McClellan on the peninsula, by the rapid movements of "Stonewall' Jackson in the Shenandoah Valley, and by the crushing defeat administered to the Union armies at Chancellorsville.

III

Now, who stood against the "Establishment" in England and on the continent? Primarily the working classes. In England they were struggling for political representation since the Reform Bill of 1833 had largely bypassed them. That act had not enfranchised the town workers; nor had it enfranchised the country laborers. The working classes were still not equal before the law. This lack of equality had caused the family of Andrew Carnegie to become Chartists; and it was one of the reasons why Carnegie himself migrated to America and why for some years when he returned to England he was an almost open preacher of republicanism and opposed to the monarchy.

The workers of Lancashire and Yorkshire were unemployed because of the lack of cotton, and many were starving. Nevertheless they gathered to adopt resolutions in support of the North, denouncing active participation in the war and advocating neutrality rather than recognition. They gathered in the humble red brick chapels of the Methodist and Baptist faiths to pray for the cause of freedom, for a united America, and for the hopes of American men and women of humble origins like their own. They did this in the way which often defied the thunder of the press and the subtleties of organized propaganda. Here on earth their prayers and the simple hymns of Isaac Watts which they sang probably did not make as many decibels of sound as the pealing organs of the cathedrals where pro-southern and anti-Lincoln sermons were uttered from the pulpit. But I believe that their quiet prayers were more in accordance with the eternal spirit than the sermons of the powerful.

Were there any others besides the working class who stood with Lincoln and the North? Yes, a few: some intellectuals and writers like Victor Hugo, self-exiled Titan; the feminist, George Sand; and John Stuart Mill, who, though the greatest economist of his time, was disliked by the fox hunters as an egghead and a do-gooder who had flirted with strange ideas in the later editions of his *Principles of Political Economy* and had been trained by the egregious radical Jeremy Bentham. Mill also was suspect because he was a Unitarian and in his youth had been arrested for distributing birth control literature.

There were stray noblemen like Richard Monckton Milnes, later Lord Houghton, of dubious personal habits but who had the grace to admire Florence Nightingale and Abraham Lincoln. And there was his young protégé, the auburn-haired Algernon Charles Swinburne, who had just published some poems in praise of Venus. There were the working class leaders such as George Howell, many of the old Chartists, and others whose presence today would call down an impeachment of the North through guilt by association.

Of the eminent political figures there was notably only one, John Bright, the Quaker radical from Rochdale. John Bright as a young man had stood with Richard Cobden and had forced Sir Robert Peel to repeal the Corn Laws and to abolish the protective tariff. He had joined with his co-religionists to feed the starving people of Ireland at the time of the potato famine. He had stood alone in the House of Commons in opposing the Crimean War despite the denunciations of a united country. He proclaimed before an awed House, after pointing to seat after seat which had been vacated by deaths and wounds through the war, his famous words, "The Angel of Death has been abroad through the land; you may almost hear the beating of his wings." Now, again almost alone, he stood for Lincoln and the North. In Parliament, on the stump throughout Great Britain though frequently threatened with lynching, in articles to the newspapers and magazines, in conversations with and letters to the leaders of the time, Bright spoke for freedom. Listen to his words at a great meeting of working men called to support the North in 1863 shortly after the Emancipation Proclamation had been formally issued:

There may be men, rich men in this city of London who will buy in the slave owner's loan and who for the chance of more gain than honest dealing will afford them, will help a conspiracy whose fundamental institutions, whose cornerstone was declared to be a felony infamous by the statutes of their own country. I speak not to these men, I leave them to their conscience in that hour which comes to all of us when conscience speaks and the soul is no longer deaf to her voice. I speak rather to you, the working men of London, the representatives as you are here tonight, of the feelings and the interests of the millions who cannot hear my voice. I wish you to be true to yourselves —Dynasties may fall, aristocracies may perish, privilege will vanish into the dim past, but you, your children and your children's children will remain and from you the English people will be continued to succeeding generations. You wish the freedom of your country, you wish it for yourselves, you strive for it in many ways. Do not then give the hand of fellowship to the worst foes of freedom that the world has ever seen. Do not, I beseech you, bring down a curse upon your cause which no act of penitence can ever lift from it. You will not do this. I have faith in this and in you. Impartial history will tell, that when your statesmen were hostile or coldly neutral, when many of your rich men were corrupt, when your press which ought to instruct and defend was mainly written to betray, the fate of a continent and of its vast population being in peril, you clung to freedom with an unfaltering trust that God and his infinite mercy will yet make it the heritage of all his children.

IV

It was this despised group which kept the faith and ultimately prevented Great Britain and France from recognizing the South. They did so first by keeping Europe neutral and then by swinging public opinion to the side of the North. Nevertheless, it would be a mistake to imagine that this was done merely or primarily by moral suasion alone. In my judgment, it could not have been done without the Union victories in the field. It was Antietam which made the European powers falter in their belief in the inevitability of southern victory. It was Antietam which taught Lord Russell and Lord Palmerston that the South was not going to win as easily as they had thought. It gave them pause as to whether they might not be backing the wrong side if they recognized the South.

Then, the next July, Gettysburg and Vicksburg made it clear that the South and slavery were indeed not going to win. Possibly the North might not win, but the South was certainly not going to win. And then the dogged persistence of the humble people of the North and the meat-chopper tactics of Grant and Sherman and that of the armies of the east and the west finally brought Union victory in the spring of 1865.

The victory at Antietam, or rather the drawn battle at Antietam, had made it possible for Lincoln to issue the Emancipation Proclamation and the war then became a moral as well as an economic and political affair. The detractors of Lincoln and of the North were put morally on the defensive, and this issue was exploited to the full by Henry Ward Beecher and Moncure Conway, while John Bright was quick to capitalize upon it.

V

Then came the final victory, the surrender of Lee, and the assassination of Lincoln. Lincoln was no longer to be feared and the North had won. It was good tactics now to praise the North; there was no further reason to be afraid of Lincoln, he had passed from the earth and so it was now safe to praise him and for men to say that they had always been on his side. *Punch,* which had been so cruel, now published a cartoon drawn by Tenniel himself of posterity laying a wreath on the bier of Abraham Lincoln. And curiously enough, someone who signed himself Tom Taylor wrote eight lines, possibly in penitence:

You lay a wreath on murdered Lincoln's bier,
You, who with mocking pencil wont to trace
Broad for the self-complacent British sneer,
His length of shambling limb, his furrowed face,
Yes, he had lived to shame me from my sneer,
To lame my pencil, and confute my pen,
To make me own this hind, of princes peer,
This railsplitter, a true-born king of men. . . .

Now it is a happy instinct on the part of mankind to allow the dead to be reconciled with their foes and to join together in happy union men who though they struggled against each other in life somehow in the process of time come to be conceived as having been allies. In my lifetime, I have seen this happen to two other noble Illinoisians who walked the long, hard road to their death amidst bitter denunciation — John Peter Altgeld, governor of Illinois for four years, who ranks only slightly below Lincoln as one of our political saints, and Jane Addams, the one authentic saint that I have ever known or seen. Cannot their experience, as well as that of Lincoln, cause us to echo the sentiments of George Bernard Shaw at the conclusion of his play "Saint Joan":

Oh, God, who has made this beautiful earth,

When will it be ready to receive Thy saints?
How long, Oh Lord, how long?

I like to think that the spirit which breathed through the souls of John Bright and Lincoln does not lie buried beneath the simple slab in the Quaker graveyard at Rochdale where Bright, in the words of George Macaulay Trevelyan, sleeps "in that humble house of peace, among his own people," nor here on this gentle slope where we do honor to Lincoln, but that it burns a little more brightly in the hearts and souls of men because of their lives and those of their true allies. All this, therefore, gives possibly some reassurance and greater faith in the instinctive judgment of the humble to those of us who live a century later. As Pascal once remarked, the heart itself has its reasons, and frequently we err in not listening to it.

The End of the Centennial

BY BRUCE CATTON

This observance is unique. I think this is the first time in history that the surviving veterans of a great war got together a full century later and spent four years celebrating their own achievements.

For complete historical accuracy, of course, it must be admitted that none of us actually fought in that war. We just feel as if we had. Sometimes we have fought about it. In any case, we have lived through it. Most of us, I suppose, began to do that long before the centennial came. And it must be added that we were all volunteers. We signed up for the duration. When the great test of the centennial came, we rallied to the flag; indeed, we rallied to both flags at once. Our patriotic fervor was leavened with a fine sense of impartiality. And we stuck to the finish. We took certain casualties along the way, some of us acquired war scars, there is a great deal of combat fatigue — but at least we saw it through. About all that remains is to find out about the pensions. We have been at it, in other words, for a long time.

A historian once advised his students that when they examined the people of any particular period in the past they should "study them until you can hear them talking." Most of us participating in this event, I suppose, have done that. We got personally acquainted with those soldiers of so long ago; got so well acquainted that we have heard them talking. They came alive for us, and we listened to them and I think we learned something thereby. In a way the whole centennial commemorative effort has been an exercise, by the entire country, in trying to hear what the men of the 1860's have to say to us.

They have had a good deal to say, and as we come now to the end of the centennial observance I think it is worth our while to sum up what we have all learned. It is time for such a summing-up. This is muster-out time — or, if you prefer, the time of parole. To paraphrase General Grant's famous sentence, we can now return to our homes, not to be disturbed by the centennial authorities so long as we observe our paroles and the laws that are in force where we reside. Before we go, however, let's look back and see what we got out of it all. What was this four-year centennial worth to the nation that sponsored it? Did we, as a country, get anything out of it worth all of the time, money, and effort that were put into it?

Perhaps the most striking single fact about this whole business, to begin with, is that our observance of the one hundredth anniversary of the Civil War is an event unique in history. When, at any time or place recorded in the annals of history, have all of the people of a proud nation gathered together, by mutual consent, to commemorate the memory of a *civil war?* That is the sort of thing that never happens. Civil wars are things people want to forget. I have never heard of Englishmen and Scotsmen getting together to make fraternal speeches on the field of Culloden, or of any great pageant staged as Naseby; or all of France pausing in its other concerns to relive the events connected with the Paris Commune in 1870; or of Irishmen and Englishmen making a pleasant holiday out of ceremonies connected with the Battle of Boyne. It just does not happen.

Civil wars are the worst of all wars. They raise memories that are best laid quitely to rest. Their effects remain as scar tissue; often enough, as a matter of fact, the wounds they create really never do heal, the hatreds and antagonisms that caused and were increased by rebellion never die out but remain generation after generation to breed a sullen anger and suspicion that at last become wholly poisonous. Never do the descendants of the contending parties find that their common memories of their time of contention are something that both sides like to relive — even to the extent of donning the old uniforms again, unfolding the old flags, and reenacting the very battles that once drove them apart. Never — except that it did work out that way with us.

The memory of our Civil War has not been a divisive force in this country. On the contrary, it has been a source of unity — something that ties us together and gives us a new depth of mutual understanding. Incredibly, the greatest and most terrible war we ever fought — the one we fought with each other — has given us greater strength and a more enduring unity. It has given us a common tradition, shared memories that go to the very roots of our existence as a people. The most remarkable single fact about the centennial observance that is now ending is that it was held at all. It was not imposed by decree or undertaken from any sense of duty. It was simply something we all wanted to do.

Shared memories of this kind are extremely important, especially in a land whose origins are as diverse as ours. Our national history is not, after all, very long, and every nation and race on earth is represented among us; yet we have not become what might have been expected from such a situation — a mere conglomeration of separate peoples, bound together by nothing much stronger than geography and the accidents of economic interest. We are perhaps the most cohesive people on earth, bound together by ties that cannot be broken or even weakened, and I believe the greatest single reason for this is our intense absorption in our own history. We have a deep and enduring consciousness of our own past; more than anything else, that is what makes us Americans. If our national tradition is comparatively brief it is extremely powerful. And the largest, most compelling, and ultimately the most consequential chapter in that historical tradition of ours is the story of our Civil War.

We look back on it for many reasons; the foremost, perhaps, is our own universal recognition that when the worst that can be said about the Civil War has been said, that war remains as the stupendous price America paid to break its way into the modern world. During the past century our country not only entered the modern world but came to lead it, almost to dominate it. It had always had a great potential; what the Civil War did was make it certain that the potential would be freed to develop to its utmost. Because of that experience of ours — so painful, acquired at such terrible expense — we found ourselves committed to a course of development unlike any other in history: we got the opportunity, along with the obligation, to develop to the utmost the infinite material capacities of modern man, hand in hand with the infinite possibilities that develop out of human freedom. Taken together, these make a powerful combination. So far we have hardly done more than scratch the surface in either of these directions, but the opportunity is still there — along with the obligation. I think great days are ahead of us.

These, to be sure, might have come anyway, without the war — later, perhaps, and in a different way.

They *did* come to us, however, from the Civil War, and that is one great reason it has been so worth our while to look back on the experience.

Now there is another angle to consider here. We agree that our experience has been blessedly unique in that we have been able to make a great asset out of something that might well have been a profound and crippling liability. How did it happen that way? What were some of the direct, tangible reasons for our quick development of this attitude? *Why* has our memory of the Civil War served to tie us together rather than to drive us apart?

Precisely here we owe something to General Ulysses S. Grant and to General Robert E. Lee. When those two men met at Appomattox a century ago they served their reunited country very well indeed. For they made, supported, and led all others to support a little document that could be the basis of a genuine peace of reconciliation. By what they did there they set the terms for the peace: No reprisals on the one hand, full acceptance of the result on the other. The thing to bear in mind here is that civil wars usually don't end that way. They bring an imposed peace that has to be supported by force for years, sometimes forever, and the settlement usually intensifies the passions that brought the trouble in the first place. It was not so at Appomattox. Grant rode back to his army and, as his first act, angrily stopped his men from firing salutes to their own success, on the commonsense ground (so very, very rare at the end of a great rebellion) that the men who had just surrendered were fellow countrymen again and ought to be accepted as such.

And Lee returned to his own army, composed a brief, temperate address telling his men to accept what had happened and to look to their future as citizens of a nation they had tried so hard to tear apart. Then he rode quietly off into legend. It is that legend that I would like to discuss briefly now.

The Confederate legend has grown mightily in the last century, until now it is a possession of the entire country, although of course it is revered most mightily in the South. It began to grow the moment Lee turned Traveller's head away from Appomattox, and it has been growing ever since, until now it is a mighty, omnipresent force in the land. You are all familiar with it. It begins with Lee, the deified man done in bronze on a bronze horse, incapable of error or human frailty, abiding forever in the Valhalla (whose membership is extraordinarily small, when you stop to think about it) of Americans who may not be criticized or questioned. And the Confederate soldier followed him into the same legend as the incredibly gallant, heroic long-suffering mortal who triumphed over fatigue, over hardship, over the terrors of battle, over everything except the force of superior numbers and who went down to defeat at last conscious that he had done all a brave man could do for a cause that was wholly unspotted. That, in its barest outline, is the legend of the Lost Cause.

Now I would like to suggest to you, in all seriousness, that this legend of the Lost Cause has been an asset to the entire country. Contrast what was with what might have been, remembering as you do that the heritage of a civil war is almost universally a heritage of bitterness and fury. The people of the South had battled to the limit of endurance for four years against a power that was at last too strong for them. They had built up a reserve of emotional involvement that could have found a most desperate outlet. The Civil War could so easily have brought about a state of incurable guerilla warfare, with eternal enmity proclaimed by crossroads ambushes and midnight reprisals, with dragoons harrying the countryside across state after state, tamping down each outburst but as the same time increasing the pressure that would evoke another explosion. Hand in hand with this would have gone unending plots and conspiracies; the war itself would have been ended, but it would not have been *settled.* An incurable sore would have been created that men would hardly even try to heal, and in the end incalculable damage would have been inflicted on the entire nation. The Civil War might very conceivably have been a tragedy from which our country could never have recovered.

That this did not happen was of course due to a large extent to Lee himself. He saw that danger, spoke against it, flatly refused to countenance any suggestion that the struggle be kept alive after the formal fighting had ended, and threw his immense influence into the scales on the side of peace and reconciliation.

But I think another important factor was the Confederate legend itself. I suspect that it became a most important channel through which the deep emotional currents that flowed across the southland were led off into a region where they could never again provoke violence. The glorification of the Lost Cause drew a great part of its strength from the fact that the loss itself was admitted and accepted. It contained no hint that enmity should be kept alive and that the wrongs of war should be avenged. It became a form of adjustment to a reality that was unpleasant; the passion that might so easily have poisoned American life forever spiraled off, or at least the major part of it did, into the enshrinement of a beautiful and romantic legend which over the years has been a most useful thing for the country as a whole. It has saved us, indirectly but effectively, a great deal of trouble.

By saying all of this I, of course, do not mean to imply that a reign of universal love and brotherhood dawned the moment the armies finished their business at Appomattox. That resentments still exist I do not doubt. That a certain emotional gap still remains between Yankees and Southerners is beyond question a fact of present-day life. What I am saying is that we did not get out of that war something that it would have been impossible to live with. We got something people could manage, something they could handle, and the very intensity of the Confederate legend has been one of the most helpful factors.

One more point remains. I believe that these centennial years have given us a new understanding of our own past and of each other, and these things are of very great importance. But during these years we have come to see one other thing more clearly than we saw it before. The war not only gave us a new base for unity and a deeper realization of the part that unity must play in our national life; it also greatly broadened the base of human freedom, and it left us with the great obligation to see that a proper edifice is built on that base. The war did end human slavery; ending it, it made all men free and left us compelled to understand that freedom in America is as indivisible as it is universal, that it is secure for the most fortunate only if at the same time it is secure for the least fortunate. Our Declaration of Independence begins with the flat assertion that all men are created equal; the Civil War closed with the flat assertion that equality has to be made good.

We study the people until we can hear them talking. One participant in the Civil War we ought to start listening to is the Negro. He was central, in that war. If his existence as a slave was not precisely the cause of the war, it was at least a factor without which the war would not have taken place. The Negro was what the war was about, somehow, and any attempt to define what the war means must take him into account. I suggest that we listen to him for a moment.

In 1863 the federal government maintained an immense concentration camp — really, there is no other word for it — somewhere in Arkansas. It was a horrible place. Anything you can find in the record about the terrors of prison camps like Andersonville or Elmira pales into nothing when compared with the record of this place. It was a fearful place of trial for people who blindly, dumbly, but led on by an indomitable hope, were trying to climb from their place below the bottom rung of the ladder. They came to this camp and were treated so badly that some of them actually elected to go back into slavery in the belief that Simon Legree could do nothing to them which would be as bad as what their liberators were doing. Some good people in the North tried to help them by sending gifts of clothing. Now it happened that these refugees from slavery had children with them, and the death rate for these children, in the unsanitary camps where they were poorly fed and given little medical care, was appalling. The people who distributed clothing to these refugees soon noticed an odd fact. When a child died (which happened all the time) the parents would take the best garments that had been given to them in order to clothe the child for burial. Those supervisors who cared about such things tried to reason with them, explaining that this clothing, after all, was for the living; the dead children would not be helped by wearing it into their graves. The Negroes understood this well enough, but their answer was unvarying: "Yes, we know, but we want them to look pretty." Study them until you can hear them talking. That way comes understanding.

Now the plight of the colored man, in and after the war, goes to the very heart of our existence as a nation. He was given the right to full freedom and equality because of the war, but this right has never been made good. This failure means that reforms must be made, not merely in some of our laws and customs, but in our own hearts as well. Because of the Civil War, we are obliged to grapple with, and to destroy, the evil of race prejudice. By removing slavery the Civil War left that evil out on the counter, naked and undisguised, and now it is ours to deal with. This is not a southern problem; all of you know very well that it is poisonous in the North as well. The job of conquering it, so that freedom and equality may be the rule everywhere in the land, is with us in Springfield as in Selma. It is the unfinished business left with us by that war whose centennial we are now closing. I suggest that it is time we got on with it.

So what is left to us, as the centennial period closes? We have what we began with: memories of a great and tragic experience. One memory that molded us as a people and left us with a great responsibility; one also that is lit with purple shadows and touched by the voices of people who lived long before we were born and who speak somehow of the America they served and loved, the America it is ours to honor. They left us, too, with a sense of mission, a realization that we have an obligation to the past and to the future which we must in the end live up to.

On the last day of his life, Good Friday, April 14, 1865, Abraham Lincoln told members of his cabinet about a strange dream he had had the night before. He dreamed, he said, that he was on a mysterious ship, moving rapidly over an uncertain sea toward what he described as "a dark and indefinite shore." He considered this an omen of some sort, and indeed it was:

He went to Ford's Theatre that night, and Booth shot him to death. The strange gift of second sight apparently came to this man, once in a while, but this one time it gave him something he could not quite interpret.

We are left just slightly in his predicament. His dream is still an omen: A full century later, we are on that mysterious vessel, moving across an uncertain sea toward a dark and indefinite shore — a shore for which there is no chart, because no man has ever seen it. Yet we do know a little something about it. It is the shore of that undiscovered country toward which America has been bound from the beginning: a country in which the noblest dreams Americans have ever had will come closer to being true simply because all of us share in them. We have had four years of looking back, now it is time to look ahead. Whether we reach the shore is up to us. We have only to live up to our past and to do our honest best to lay our hands on the magnificent future which that past lights up for us.

The Centennial of Lincoln's Burial

BY ADLAI E. STEVENSON

On this quiet hillside just a century ago, the fearful journey ended. "The night came with great quiet" and the noble heart was laid to rest.

Bishop Matthew Simpson addressed the thousands of mourners who had accompanied the remains of their dear friend and neighbor to this, his final resting place. He was eloquent and, as was expected in those days, he was long — he spoke for over one hour — beginning his biographical remarks with the phrase, "Mr. Lincoln was no ordinary man." As the Bishop drew his address to a close, he echoed the words that had been spoken across the country during the almost three weeks since the President's death: "Let us resolve to carry forward the policy which he so nobly began. Let us do right to all men."

This alone was Lincoln's aim when he loosed the lightning stroke that declared the slaves "forever free." Now, one hundred years after the guns of fratricidal war were silenced, one hundred years after Lincoln's voice was stilled, the promise has not yet been redeemed in full. America is still paying for the "bondsman's 250 years of unrequited toil." For the chains were replaced by other bonds. And, until those are finally loosed, the task that Lincoln began is not finished.

No, the task is not finished; the lingering legacy of those distant days of anguish is still at work, dividing and demeaning us. And that is why one still hears haunting echoes of those deathless words: "With malice toward none; with charity for all." In his address to the Congress on civil rights, for example, President Lyndon Johnson insists that: "None of us in any section look with prideful righteousness on the troubles in another section as the problems of our neighbors."

Lincoln saw human affairs and human emotions in all their complexity and ambiguity and, if ever a leader lived by the biblical inspiration, "Judge not, lest ye be judged," it was this man who groped his way to the sense of Divine Providence, and wrestled all the time with the doubts that must beset minds that can see more than one facet of truth. He never stopped feeling that he did not have all the answers.

And that is the condition of wisdom; that is what made him the least pompous and most lovable of politicians.

My old friend Carl Sandburg once said that the Civil War was fought over a verb. Before the war people said, "The United States *are* . . ." and, after 1865, "The United States *is*. . . ." Sandburg may have been premature in his use of the second verb. But, today, who can doubt any longer the resolution of the vast majority of the people of the United States to achieve that unity and, in Lincoln's words, "to finish the work we are in."

In a century, we have resolved many of our sectional differences. As Bruce Catton reminds us the Civil War now, in a way, unites us by providing both North and South with a common memory. The bitterness of that terrible struggle is gone and now, a century later, we can lay what few differences still exist to rest alongside the great son of Illinois who sleeps here.

One hundred years of remembrance are ended on this day. The Civil War Centennial is over. A new century begins.

Let us look forward to the new century. And let us begin today to improve the *quality* of our society, and be in *fact* the exemplars of democracy for the world. The spirit of democracy is moral. It emphasizes *right* as well as rights, and *responsibilities* as well as *freedoms*.

In these, *our* dark days of fear and strife, we can again give hope and courage to sorrowing, suffering masses from the Mississippi to the Mekong if we heed

Lincoln's admonition "to do all which may achieve and cherish a just and lasting peace among ourselves and with all nations."

Speaking to Congress one hundred and three years ago, he said: "We can succeed only by concert. It is not 'can *any* of us *imagine* better?' but 'can we *all do* better?' "

I can best conclude my remarks as he did his: "The way is plain, peaceful, generous, just — a way which, if followed, the world will forever applaud, and God must forever bless."

Finally, my friends, *we* shall not be the *last* to stand here at Lincoln's venerated tomb, because countless men and women will, like Walt Whitman, mourn him "with ever-returning spring."